LettsGuide

SO-BUD-870

Portugal

Harold Dennis-Jones

First published 1974
by Charles Letts and Company Limited
Diary House, Borough Road, London SE1 1DW
Revised 1977, 1979, 1980
Designed by Ed Perera
Cover: Photograph: J Allan Cash Limited
Photographs: Harold Dennis-Jones (p 56)
A F Kersting, London (pp 28, 46)
Portuguese National Tourist Office (pp 45, 55, 66)
Illustrations: Ed Perera (pp 3, 63, 75)

© Text: Harold Dennis-Jones
ISBN 0 85097 431 3

Printed in Great Britain by
Charles Letts (Scotland) Limited

Charles Letts & Co Ltd
London, Edinburgh, München & New York

Contents

What this book is all about

This little book sets out to do three main things. It tries to tell you enough about what you can see and do in Portugal and about the people you will meet there to enable you to decide where you want to go and what you want to do. It gives you an outline of how to travel to and in Portugal, so that you can decide your own routes. And it indicates costs sufficiently clearly to allow you to budget your visit accurately enough.

The book does not go lengthily into detailed accounts of what you ought to do and what you ought to see and how much exactly each item will cost.

Sensible travellers make up their own minds—and, anyway, finding the final details out for yourself and making your own choices constitutes one of travel's major excitements.

But if time and money is limited, as it is for nearly everyone, you will need guidance. That is what we aim to give. And wherever possible we try to tell you where you can get more up-to-date and fuller information both before you go and after your arrival. This applies specially, of course, to prices, which change continuously nowadays.

We would like to think that everything in this book is perfect. But we know there will be mistakes because we ourselves are anything but perfect. If you find any errors, be kind. Please write and tell us about them, so that at least we can avoid misleading future readers.

Have a good trip!

Facts at your fingertips

Travel preparations

Travel documents

To enter Portugal for up to 60 days British Citizens need either a full passport or the British Visitor's Passport obtainable quickly at all principal Post Offices. Americans and Canadians need a passport. All necessary information, including passport application forms, can be obtained at Post Offices in all three countries. Various formalities (birth certificate or previous passport or other proof of identity, certified passport-size photographs, etc) are necessary, so begin the enquiry/application process well ahead of travel dates—several months if possible for full passports. In the USA first-time-ever applications involve a personal appearance before one of a wide range of specified officials. Most travel agents will help and advise.

In the UK and USA, but not in Canada, a wife can be included on her husband's passport and vice versa. In all three countries children under 16 can be included on a parent's passport. In such cases the passport cannot be used in the holder's absence.

Health

Provided you have not been in possible contact with serious infections such as smallpox or cholera there are no compulsory vaccinations. You may however wish to protect yourself against tetanus (if you have not already done so) and infectious hepatitis, which occurs in some Mediterranean areas. Your doctor will do what is needed, but allow time for ordering the vaccines.

Take a supply of any medicaments you use regularly adequate to last your stay (they will not necessarily be available in Portugal). Take also sun lotion to deal with strong sun if you are not regularly used to it, an antiseptic cream and a little plaster for small open wounds, aspirin or something similar for headaches, and anti-motion sickness pills if you suffer that way. Stomach upsets occur easily in a warm climate accompanied by unaccustomed food and maybe more drink than usual. Avoiding all fats or even keeping the stomach empty for 24 hours (except for water) is often the best cure. But ask your pharmacist's or doctor's advice if you want a specific against tummy upsets.

Insurance

Travel mishaps are thankfully scarce, but can be unbelievably expensive when they do occur. All travellers should insure themselves against loss of deposits paid to airlines, tour operators, hotels, and the like through their own or a near relative's illness or death in the family, etc. They need also insurance against the sometimes huge costs of special air tickets home for themselves and perhaps a companion, extra hotel costs, etc, following accident or illness abroad.

No free medical treatment is available in Portugal, and doctors' and hospitals' fees can be high. This sounds grim but insurance costs little. In *Britain* many tour operators and most insurance companies have standard 'travel policies'. The AA, RAC, Caravan Club, and Camping Club of Great Britain arrange cover for members. Europ Assistance provides special medical and other help including an advice centre in London that never closes (phone or use the hotel telex), has air and road ambulances with qualified attendants constantly available to bring you home in serious cases, and maintains on-the-spot agents who not only help and advise but also guarantee payments without your having to find possibly large sums of ready cash. Europ Assistance is closely linked with similar organisations in most West European countries, and their related company Europa Insurance provides non-medical cover. But shop around and find a policy that suits your particular needs.

US and Canadian citizens should consult their travel agents and insurance companies or agents about any travel insurance they need. In Canada Ontario Blue Cross provides short-term foreign medical cover, and Voyageur Travel Insurance looks after everything. In the States CIEE looks after students. IAMAT (International Association for Medical Assistance to Travellers) issues lists of English-speaking doctors familiar with North American medical practice in return for a small membership fee. The World Medical Association gives similar help. The US Consumers' Union publishes a traveller's health guide.

Money
The easiest way of carrying money is in the form of traveller's cheques, obtainable from banks (not necessarily your own) and travel-banking firms such as the universally known Thomas Cook or American Express. Traveller's cheques are useful because they can be cashed almost anywhere, are accepted by many hotels, shops, airlines, etc, can usually be refunded on the spot if lost (check this when buying them), and are not easily used by other people if stolen. In the UK buy them for preference from the 'High Street' banks, in the USA from Bank of America, Citibank, or Perera, and in Canada from the Bank of Montreal, the Canadian Imperial Bank of Commerce, etc. Apart from Thomas Cook and American Express of course.

However much they dislike it, Canadians may find it best to buy cheques in US dollar denominations. In remoter spots Canadian dollars may not be readily accepted. At times of severe currency fluctuation it is always possible to buy cheques in a stable currency —Swiss francs, say, or Dutch florins, or West German marks.

Major international credit cards like Diners, Visa, American Express, Master Charge, etc can be used to buy airline tickets, car hire, accommodation, meals, and maybe goods (mostly in more expensive establishments), and are specially useful in emergencies.

UK residents holding Eurocheque and bank (but not Visa) cards are usually allowed to cash personal cheques of up to £30 twice per day in European banks. Visa cardholders can cash one personal cheque of up to £50 per day in branches of Barclay's or banks displaying the Visa sign. Notify your bank of cheques cashed in this way. American Express cardholders can obtain up to $500 in cash from American Express offices in a period of 21 days.

No one leaving the UK is allowed to take out more than £100-worth of British banknotes, nor more than £500-worth of British and other banknotes combined.

Package tours
In a country which you do not know a package tour is an attractive proposition. Packages nowadays need not by any means involve your being constantly shepherded around or dumped in a single large hotel with a large group. Coach tours through more than one European country are still admittedly popular. But more and more tours are nowadays deliberately designed to give you as much individual freedom and choice as possible. Yet all offer one dominating advantage—you make a single payment and leave someone else to bother about virtually all the practical chores like travel and hotel bookings, transfers, etc.

From North America Just to give some idea of the choice available, relaxation and touring holidays in Portugal are provided by the following North American firms: American Express, Caravan, Globus-Gateway, Tourvac, Maupintour, Olson, Overseas Travel, Percival Tours, Travel-Go-Round, CP Air, TWA Getaway, UTL, and others. Golf holidays can be had through B & J Tours, CP Air, International Golf, etc. Catholic Travel and Destination World are two of the main companies organising religious tours. Fly-drive is provided by Atesa Marsans, Europcar, and other firms. Some of these holidays are outstandingly cheap. Help and advice is available from Portuguese National Tourist Offices.

From UK the choice, as you would expect, is even wider, and includes a large variety of self-catering holidays in villas and flats, which many people find ideal for families. For general sun-and-sand holidays try: Travel Club, Flair, Sovereign, Enterprise, Global, Thomson, Thomas Cook, Wings, etc. Those providing self-catering holidays include: Algarve Villas, Beach Villas, Meon Travel, OSL, Travel Club, Villas Portuguesas, and others. Firms offering motoring holidays include: British Airways Freewheeler, Thomas Cook, TAP, and others. Speical interest tours range from architecture and art to such things as bird-watching, golf and other sports. Academy, Swans, Global, Travel Club, John Morgan, and others organise holidays of this type. Inter-Church and other firms take pilgrims to Fatima. But this is by no means a full list. Consult your travel agent and, if necessary, the Portuguese National Tourist Office in London.

More information

Already at this stage you will be wanting more information than can possibly be crammed into any book. **In Britain** your best sources are a good local travel agent and the Portuguese Tourist Office in London. Three Portuguese NTOs serve the **USA** and there are two in **Canada**. In addition to what good US or Canadian travel agents can do to help you, airlines operating to Portugal are also pretty knowledgeable. But if you are writing or calling, try to make your questions specific. Embassies and Consulates provide information about cultural, educational, and specialised professional matters

Bookings

However you decide to travel (except on special student tickets) there can be solid advantages in making as many bookings as possible through a local travel agent. It costs nothing, uses an expert's knowledge (if you choose your agent carefully), and saves time and trouble. If difficulties arise over changed arrangements or the like the travel agent can advise and usually also help. In the USA and Canada most agents are capable also—for a fee— of designing itineraries, booking hotels, and so on for fully independent tours. In Britain, with a few exceptions, only firms handling business travel expect to do this.

Climate and clothes

Thanks to the Gulf Stream and the nearness of the Atlantic, Portugal has a generally mild climate, even in the country's cooler northern half. In the south, along both the west-facing and south-facing coasts the climate is Mediterranean—that is, with dry warm summers and mild winters—despite the fact that these shores face the Atlantic. Rain, sometimes heavy and prolonged, falls mainly between November and February. Spring comes early, especially in the south. Summers are distinctly hot by northern standards, but not unpleasantly so. Among the inland northern hills and on the high Serra da Estrela, winter is, of course, colder than on the coast, and in the south occasional high winds are possible in summer, even when the weather is completely dry. Most visitors find the Portuguese climate extremely pleasant.

Leisure clothes can be worn all the time on the Algarve coast. In Lisbon and the more expensive hotels in Oporto, Cascais, Estoril, and similar places, formal suits and dresses should be taken for the evenings. The Portuguese are still inclined to be rather proper. While no rules are laid down, they prefer visitors to wear 'modest' clothing when visiting churches—trousers, not shorts, for men and not over-skimpy clothes for women. Away from main tourist centres they are even apt to be a little offended if they find tourists wearing what they consider unsuitable dress, whether over-bright or over-brief.

Getting to Portugal—and back

From UK you can reach Portugal by air or by through train services. If you are taking your own car see Motoring.

From North America you can fly or travel by sea.

Air routes from UK
British Airways (BA for short) and Portuguese Airways (TAP) both operate direct flights daily from London (Heathrow) to Lisbon all year round. In summer one or other airline flies direct to Faro nearly every day and there are also fairly frequent flights to Oporto. British Caledonian calls at Lisbon on the way back from South America, but not outward-bound.

The usual chaos rules air fares between the two countries. There are full-rate 1st- and economy-class returns available, together with economy excursions valid from 7 days to a month. In addition there are cheaper advance-booking fares (tickets paid for a month ahead: no alterations allowed: multiples of 1 to 8 weeks only). You can also buy, sometimes from provincial airports as well as London, cheap tickets sold under various brand-names but known in the trade by the generic term 'minimun-rated packages'. Technically and legally (under international European-region air travel regulations) these are package tours. But you are not obliged to use the sometimes minimal accommodation provided. Consult a good travel agent.

From North America fares are even more complicated. You can choose between full-rate 1st-and economy-class roundtrips, economy excursion roundtrips, GITs of various sorts (for groups of minimum size: the travel agent can find the other people), cheaper APEX (Advanced Passenger Excursion) tickets which have to be booked and paid for a specified period in advance and carry restrictions limiting stopovers, cancellation refunds, etc, and a few even cheaper charters. All types of ticket have advantages and disadvantages. The small-print conditions are very complex. Consult a reliable and knowledgeable travel agent.

TAP Portuguese Airlines fly from New York to Oporto via Lisbon; from Boston to Lisbon with a stop in the Azores; and from Montreal to Lisbon with an Azores stop. TWA operate a service linking Albuquerque, Chicago, and New York with Lisbon. CP Air fly Toronto-Montreal-Lisbon.

By sea from North America
The two Yugoslav lines Jadranska Slobodna Plovidba and Jadrolinija link respectively Montreal and Quebec, and New York, Philadelphia, Newport News, Norfolk, and Baltimore, with Lisbon.

Through rail routes from UK
From London the rail-and-boat overland journey to Lisbon takes 38-43 hours. A change is necessary at Paris, and also at Irún on the French-Spanish frontier, unless you travel by the Puerta del Sol (Sun Gate) express between Paris and Madrid or the through train via Valladolid to Lisbon. For the Peurta del Sol you pay an inclusive charge covering the 1st- or 2nd-class sleeper or 2nd-class couchette, dinner and breakfast. Prices are very reasonable. From Madrid fast expresses are available to Lisbon.

The French Sud Express (Paris-Irún) connects at Irún with fast through trains to Lisbon and Oporto. Information is available in UK from BR Travel Centres and in the USA and Canada from Britrail or French National Railroads offices.

From the rest of Europe You can travel by rail easily enough from other European countries to Portugal. You have to go through Spain of course. The simplest points to make for are either Madrid or Irún, though entering Spain at Port Bou at the Pyrenees' eastern end could be more interesting. Information can be obtained as above.

Rail Bargains Special-rate tickets make combined rail tours of Portugal and other countries very economical. An InterRail card entitles UK residents aged up to 22 to a month's half-rate travel in UK and Eire, half-fare on Sealink ferries, and free rail travel in 18 other countries, including Portugal. North American residents of any age can buy a 1st-class Eurailpass providing unlimited free rail travel for varying periods in 13 European countries including Portugal, together with reductions on certain non-rail travel

services. North American residents under 26 can get the 2nd-class
Eurail Youthpass, which provides unlimited rail travel and the same
non-rail travel service reductions in the same 13 countries,
including Portugal. Information can be had in UK from British
Rail Continental HQ and BR Travel Centres, and in North
America from Britrail or French National Railroads (who also sell
Portuguese rail tickets).

Customs—what you can take into Portugal
All visitors may import into Portugal without paying Customs duty
everything intended for bona fide personal use, such as clothing,
toilet articles, jewellery, and so on, 250 g (about 9 oz) of tobacco
and tobacco goods (ie, 200 cigarettes, or 100 cigarillos, or 50 cigars),
small quantities of toilet water or perfume for personal use. 1 litre
of wine and 1 bottle of spirit (liquor) are also allowed in without
payment of duty, as are used cameras, sports equipment and
camping gear, a child's pushchair, binoculars, radio, tape recorder,
musical instruments, record player, portable TV, and portable
typewriter.

What you can bring back On their return, UK residents over 17 may
import duty-free purchases of 1 litre of strong spirits *or* 2 litres of
fortified or sparkling wine, and an additional 2 litres of still table
wine; and 200 cigarettes *or* 100 cigarillos *or* 50 cigars *or* 250 g
tobacco. Whatever their age they may also import 50 g of perfume
and $\frac{1}{4}$ litre toilet water, and £10 worth of gifts. Gifts are increased to
£50 and other items by 50% if they were purchased in ordinary
shops and normal tax paid in an EEC country such as France or
Belgium (eg if you drive back), provided you return direct from
that country. In case of doubt or difficulty consult the Customs
London HQ.

On returning to the USA you can import, without paying duty,
bona fide gifts to a value of $300, provided you have not done this
within the previous six months. You can also import a vehicle such
as a car, boat, or plane, provided it travels with you. If you are
over 21 *and your gateway State allows* (check beforehand) you can
bring in 1 US quart (.946 litre) of alcoholic drink (wine, beer, or
liquor regardless of alcohol content). 200 cigarettes or 50 cigars or
3 lb of smoking tobacco, or proportional quantities, also come in
duty-free, as do all your normal personal effects such as clothing
and jewellery. In addition, while abroad you can mail bona fide
gifts other than tobacco or alcoholic drink to a value of $25 each,
provided you label each present 'Unsolicited gift'. In case of
doubt or difficulty consult US Customs HQ.

If you are returning to Canada After 7 days or more abroad Canadian residents of any age, even babies, may import gifts worth CA$150, together with 50 cigars, 200 cigarettes, and 2 lb tobacco. They may also mail personal gifts, each under $15 in value (mark covers 'Unsolicited gift—value under $15'). Those above the age fixed by their gateway province, usually 18 or 19, may also import without paying duty 40 fl oz of wine or liquor or 24 pints of beer. For fuller details ask at your departure airport or quay for the Canada Customs brochure 'I Declare . . .': also for the booklet of advice to travellers 'Bon Voyage But . . .'. In case of doubt or difficulty about what you may be charged duty on, consult a Canada Customs office.

When you are in Portugal

NB Check airport departure taxes with your travel agent or tour operator. They are often included in package holiday prices and sometimes in other air bookings. If not, make certain you have enough local currency to pay for them before your return flight.

Getting around
Portugal has a well-developed transport system, with two domestic air routes from Lisbon, trains serving all the main areas, and buses and long-distance coaches reaching even the smallest villages, though not necessarily very frequently. Trams and/or buses and, in Oporto, trolleybuses operate in the towns. Taxis are readily available in towns and resorts. So are hire cars.

Domestic air services Lisbon-Oporto and Lisbon-Faro: two services daily on each route.

Trains Main lines run northward from Lisbon to Coimbra, Aveiro, and Oporto; south to the Algarve; and east and north-east to the Spanish frontier at Marvão and Vilar Formoso. International express to Madrid and Irún run on the last two routes. Branch lines reach to various parts of the interior. Long-distance trains are hauled by diesel locomotives and are comfortable.

In addition there are frequent electric short-distance services from Lisbon (Rossio) to Sintra and the north, and from Lisbon (Cais do Sodré) to Estoril and Cascais. Trains for the Algarve and the south start from Barreiro Station south of the Tagus. You reach it by the Sul e Sueste ferries that start from beside Lisbon's 'Black Horse Square' (Praça do Comercio). Trains have 1st- and 2nd-class coaches. Fares are not high.

'Kilometer tickets', valid for 5 months, give 5000 km of travel at reduced rate. 'Tourist tickets' provide unlimited travel for 5, 10, or 15 days. Those over 65 at all times pay half-fare.

Railway enthusiasts may like to know that a narrow-gauge 'Historical Train', with rolling-stock dating from 1881-1908 and a wide-gauge '19th Century Train' (1875-91) still make outings for parties.

Long-distance coach Coach routes between main towns are comfortable and provide a very good way of seeing the country. Fares are roughly the same as for trains.

Town buses, trams, and trolleybuses Vehicles are comfortable and services reasonably frequent; Trams and British-built double-deckers operate in Lisbon, and trams, buses and trolleybuses in Oporto. Fares vary slightly according to distance; but basically there is a set price however far you go. Lisbon boasts a fairly extensive modern underground system. It has a fixed charge.

Boats and ferries Passenger services are all cheap, even the 1-hour journey from Peniche to Berlenga Island.

Taxis Portuguese taxis are efficient and usually quite comfortable. Prices vary somewhat from region to region but are not particularly high. An extra charge is made for the use of 6-seater vehicles, but nothing extra needs be paid at night. Prices for regular journeys—for instance, from town centre to airport or outlying hotel—are officially fixed and there is no need to bargain. It is however legally obligatory to get into taxis from the pavement (sidewalk) side. Entering a vehicle from the road side makes you liable to an on-the-spot fine.

Hire Cars Self-drive cars can be hired in Portugal by the hour, day, week, or month in most places where there is a fair number of tourists. However it is well worth making arrangements in advance if possible. This is best done through the organisation you travel by —airline, travel agent, and so on—or through an international car-hire concern such as Avis, Hertz, etc. Firms in both UK and North America offer 'Fly-drive' package holidays that include air fares and car hire, with hotel reservations if required. Consult a Portuguese National Tourist Office.

Where to stay
Hotel accommodation of various types, guesthouses, motels, self-catering villas and apartments, and Youth Hostels are available in Portugal. (For campsites see Motoring). Compared with the rest of the world, prices are mostly very modest, though a few de luxe establishments on the Algarve coast and in Lisbon are rather pricey in the high season.

Those on the coast, however, reduce their rates by 15% from November to February. But if you stay in a guesthouse for more than two days and do not take your meals there the room price may be increased by 20%. All prices quoted by hotels, etc include service and tax. No tips are necessary, but are not refused by the staff.

All accommodation is officially inspected and graded. Five types of hotel-style establishment are recognised: hotels (*hoteis*), *pousadas*, *albergarias*, *pensões*, *estalagens*, and motels. The different types are distinguished chiefly by their public rooms and by the services they offer.

Hotels are divided into 5 classes, with one to five stars. One-star establishments are simple, and relatively few rooms have private baths or showers. In the two-star category every bedroom has a private bath or shower: and above that all rooms have private baths (tubs) as well as showers.

Pousadas are State-run inns, strategically located to serve motor tourists. They vary in size and type. Some occupy modern buildings: others are housed in beautifully-modernised ancient palaces and convents, such as those at Estremoz, Évora and Óbidos. One or two are fairly simple, but all are elegantly furnished with typical local handicraft-work. Prices are mostly very low. Between June 1st and October 31st your maximum stay is limited to 5 days. From November 1st to May 31st there is no limit to how long you stay in pousadas with over 10 rooms, but you cannot stay more than 7 days in those with 5-10 rooms, and 5 days in those with under 5 rooms. Very early booking is absolutely essential—and well worth the effort if you want a thoroughly enjoyable tour of the country.

Estalagens, divided into five- and four-star categories, are privately owned inns that fill roughly the same needs as the pousadas, but do not ever have the magnificent settings of the best pousadas.

Guesthouses (*pensões:* sing pensão) are awarded one to four stars according to their standards. Those with four stars normally have every room with private bath: three-star establishments have a high proportion of private baths. Public rooms and services, naturally, are simpler than hotels.

Albergarias are specially comfortable four-star *pensões*. While many of these various guesthouses are extremely simple, their service is always willing and they provide very good value for money. Many occupy only the upper floors of modern buildings.

Motels are given either three or two stars and are not very numerous. They serve fairly strictly as overnight stopping-places for motorists. Their facilities do not always include restaurants, though they serve breakfasts.

All hotels have lists of the prices permitted for each room, which they are obliged to show guests on request. They also have regularly-inspected Complaints Books, in which you can write comments if you wish.

Portuguese National Tourist offices have lists of hotels of all types and can help and advise you in your choice.

Villas and apartments Large numbers of villas and apartments are available for letting, especially in or near all main Algarve coast resorts. In standard they vary from the merely comfortable to the thoroughly luxurious, and prices tend to be fairly high—though not frighteningly so. It may sometimes be possible to arrange a let at somewhat lower rates through an office in Portugal but it is very much easier to rent through companies based in UK or North America. If you pay more it is because you get the services of on-the-spot English-speaking staff as well as a reasonable assurance that the accommodation satisfies the standards you are used to.

Letting prices are quoted either inclusive of air transport and transfers between airport and villa, or for accommodation only, in which case you make all your own travel arrangements. Maid service for specified times—often six days a week—is normally included.

Youth Hostels There are some 15 hostels, situated at strategic points. Some open only in summer, and may cater for only one sex. Those under 30 pay much less for overnights than those above that age. Breakfast and main meal, when available, are very reasonable in price. Standards are in general acceptable, though a little lower perhaps than in the best European Hostels. Further information can be obtained from your national Youth Hostels Association, which you should join before using Portuguese Hostels.

Anyone not familiar with Europe's highly-developed Youth Hostel system should realise that the non-profitmaking Hostels provide beds, possibly several to a room, washing and cooking facilities, and sometimes simple meals at the lowest possible prices. Guests themselves do the cleaning each morning, and wash up after meals.

Where to eat
Portugal can boast a splendid range of restaurants—from the sophisticatedly gourmet palaces of Lisbon and Faro to the solidly middle-class (and very Portuguese) eating-places of towns and cities large and small, the fishnet-and-bottle-bedecked tourist haunts of the Algarve coast (some of them excellent), down to the modest *tascas* patronised by ordinary village folk and discerning visitors. Whatever category you opt for, you get excellent value.

All Portuguese restaurants are officially inspected and graded into four classes— de luxe, first, second, and third. They are compelled by law to display menus and prices outside the establishments. Towns and tourist resorts usually offer a good choice of eating places. However, they are less frequent in smaller spots. In case of need, all hotels, *pousadas, estalagens* and motels welcome non-residents. If you are using them, note that their mealtimes are usually 12.00 or 12.30 to 14.00 or 14.30, and 19.30 or 20.00 to 21.00 or 23.00 (later in big towns). Breakfast is normally served from 08.00 on, rarely earlier. Many restaurants serve fixed-price *table d'hôte* (blue plate) meals that may include up to six courses.

For Portugal's culinary delights, see Life Portuguese Style.

When you are thirsty
Bars are rather more frequent than restaurants. They serve coffee (in tourist areas tea as well) and soft drinks, in additon to wine and spirits. Prices vary from low to very low except for imported drinks (such as whisky) and in top-grade hotel bars. See also Life Portuguese Style.

For your evening's entertainment
See Entertainment and Traditional Festivals, below, in Life Portuguese Style.

You and your money
Portugal's currency unit is the escudo (abbreviated $), which is divided into 100 centavos. Banknotes (bills) come in denominations of 20, 50, 100, 500 and 1000 escudos. Coins have values of $10, $20, $50, 1$00, 2$50, 5$00, 10$00 and 20$00.

Note how prices are written. 1$50 means 1 escudo 50 centavos. 25$00 means 25 escudos. But $25 means 25 centavos. Note too that small change is sometimes scarce. You may think it worth while to acquire a small stock early on and not part with too much of it needlessly.

You can take as much foreign currency and traveller's cheques into Portugal as you wish, but not more than 5000$00 in Portuguese currency. When leaving the country anyone over 18 can take with him 1000$ in Portuguese banknotes (bills) and coins, and up to 20,000$00-worth of foreign notes and coin, provided he can prove he brought this into the country.

Traveller's cheques, sterling notes, and dollar bills, can be changed easily at most banks, some travel agents, larger hotels (provided you are staying there), at the Rossio Station in Lisbon and at special exchange offices (*cambios*). Bank procedures are apt to be long-winded outside main tourist regions: use the exchange offices if possible. These also have longer opening hours—one or two in Lisbon even stay open all night. Take your passport when changing money.

Information after arrival
Visitors can get information, advice, and sometimes also help, from local Tourist Information Offices in almost every town of any importance throughout Portugal. Just look for the signs saying 'Turismo'. Hotel concierges, campsite wardens, etc are also of course helpful and knowledgeable.

The ▉ sign is used throughout Europe to indicate Tourist Information Offices which all provide free information and in some cases also make on-the-spot room bookings.

Organising your sightseeing
Coach excursions are run from all major tourist resorts and from Lisbon. But some of the pleasantest trips are those you organise for yourself—by bus, for instance, or maybe by persuading a local fisherman to take you out in his boat to see something of the coast. The local Turismo office, your hotel concierge, etc will give you all the help and advice you need.

Practical details

Children present no problems in Portugal. Under 8 they are everywhere entitled to a 50% reduction on meal prices. In hotels you pay 35% of the normal price for an extra bed in the parents' room (25% in cheaper establishments, and only half the full rate for a child under 8). Children under 4 years old travel free on trains and buses. From 4 to 12 they pay half-fare and are entitled to a seat. Babyfoods common in Europe and North America *can* be bought in the larger centres. But availability is uncertain, and it is best to bring your own supplies. Most hotels will arrange for babysitters.

Correspondence addressed to you at Posta-Restante, followed by the name of the town and province, will be held till you call to collect it (take your passport). Thomas Cook and American Express also accept your letters if you are travelling with them (or hold an American Express Card). US and Canadian Embassies hold letters addressed to their nationals for a limited time, but have no forwarding arrangements. Allow 5-6 days for letters for Portugal from UK or North America.

Dry cleaning is looked after efficiently by most town and resort hotels. But there is no shortage of cleaners in even small towns.

Electricity is mostly 220 volts, 50 cycles. Do not rely on the less expensive hotels having shaver sockets.

Emergencies Dial 115 for fire, police, ambulance, etc. If using English speak *very* slowly and use only vital words (eg, 'Accident. Serious. Here'). For less immediate worries, if you are travelling on a package tour consult the tour company's representative, or your hotel reception staff, campsite warden, etc., or the nearest Thomas Cook or American Express office if you have booked through them. Report thefts and losses promptly to the police and obtain a certificate of having done so (your insurance company will want to see it). Similarly, keep carefully for your insurance company receipts for money spent because of illness or accident.

For other problems (if you lose your passport or are arrested, for instance) contact your own Embassy or nearest Consular representative. Consular and diplomatic staff cannot supply money or make bookings for you, whatever your need. But they can give advice, inform your family, help you cable for additional funds, give you names and addresses of lawyers, and so on.

Language English is widely spoken—but not as widely as all that. You will have no trouble in main resorts and large towns. Elsewhere, a very little Portuguese goes a long way. French is sometimes spoken by older professional people.

Lavatories (Mens' and Ladies' rooms) Go into any bar or snackbar and ask for the *toilette* (pronounced roughly as in French). No need to buy anything. If there is an attendant, she is paid. Except in the remotest areas lavatories, like everything else in Portugal, are very clean. Apart from *toilette* the signs may say: *WC*, *lavabo* or *retrete*. Ladies is *Senhoras,* Gentlemen is *Homens*.

Museums and art galleries Most museums and art galleries open from 10.00 (occasionally 09.00 or 11.00) to 17.00, sometimes with a break at lunchtime (maximum 12.00-14.00 but usually less). They close mostly only on Monday (occasionally Tuesday) and on public holidays. Admission may be free on Saturday and/or Sunday.

Oranges—Beware! Don't pick the oranges! Even if you're as excited as most tourists from temperate climates are at seeing oranges actually growing on trees, do not pick those you see in public places such as streets and squares. The fruit here is reserved for distribution to needy families and there is a hefty fine, payable on the spot, for unauthorised scrumping of local authorities' fruit.

Photography There are no special restrictions, but you obviously should not point your camera at military installations or personnel. Popular types of film are sometimes available, but are rather expensive.

Places of Worship Anglican churches in Lisbon and Oporto hold services every Sunday: in Estoril most Sundays. The Church of Scotland has services every Sunday in Lisbon. Catholic services are held in English every Sunday in Lisbon and occasionally elsewhere. There are synagogues in Lisbon and Oporto. For other denominations enquire from National Tourist and local Turismo Offices.

Post Offices are mostly open during normal shopping hours. You can buy stamps from hotel concierges or reception clerks and from shops authorised to sell tobacco, as well as from Post Offices. Letterboxes are painted red.

Public holidays New Year's Day (1 January); Portuguese National Day (25 April); Labour Day (1 May); Corpus Christi (varies); National Day (10 June); Assumption (15 August); Anniversary of the Declaration of the Republic (5 October); All Saints' Day (1 November); Independence Day (1 December); Feast of the Immaculate Conception (8 December); Christmas Day (25 December). Though not officially holidays, Shrove Tuesday (the Tuesday before the start of Lent), Maundy Thursday (Thursday before Good Friday), and Good Friday are treated as such by lots of people. Many shops close on these days. Note that Easter Monday and Boxing Day are not official holidays.

Shopping and banking hours Most shops are open daily except Sundays from 09.00 to 13.00 and from 15.00 to 18.00. Local times vary however, with shops in smaller towns and tourist centres opening earlier and closing later. All shops close on national holidays, and on some local holidays. See Festivals, below, in Life Portuguese Style.

Banks are open 09.00 to 12.00 and 14.00 to 15.30 on Monday to Friday, apart from public holidays and local festival days.

Telephones Dialling is automatic to most places inside Portugal. Calls can be made from very British-looking call boxes, but it is usually easier (except perhaps in Lisbon) to go into any bar and pay a little more. You are not expected to buy drinks when making phone calls.

Time Portugal's clock time is the same as Britain's in both summer and winter, and is similarly 5 hours ahead of North America Eastern Time. Air timetables always show local time. Confusion occurs because all three territories introduce summer Daylight Saving Time at different dates (mid-March to late-April) and end it between late September and late October. Check carefully if you are travelling at these periods.

Tipping While there is no need to tip in hotels or restaurants where a service percentage is added, remember that Portuguese earnings are still very low. Tips are appreciated, even if modest. Give chambermaids and hotel concierges who have been helpful 50-100$00 for a week. Hotel baggage porters get 10-20$00, railway and airport porters 5$00 per bag and a bit extra, cloakroom attendants 3-5$00, theatre and cinema usherettes 2-3$00, taxi drivers 15%, hair-dressers 10% (minimum 10$00), bars and places where service charge is not included at least 10%, where it is included 5-10%.

Youth and student travel There are a few special facilities or price reductions. Consult a specialised student travel organisation or a Portuguese National Tourist Office if necessary. Ordinary prices anyway are at least as low as young travellers can get elsewhere in Europe.

Essential addresses

For ferry companies operating from UK, airlines based in the country you are starting from, and tour operators, it is best to consult a good local travel agent. He has up-to-date information, and will usually be able to answer queries, make bookings, etc.

In Britain Portuguese National Tourist Office, New Bond Street House, 15 New Bond Street, London W1

Portuguese Embassy, 11 Belgrave Square, London SW1

TAP Portuguese Airlines, Gillingham House, 38-44 Gillingham Street, London SW1V 1JW

British Rail Continental, PO Box 2, Victoria Station, London SW1V 6YL

AA, PO Box 50, Basingstoke Hants, RT21 2ED

Camping Club of Great Britain, 11 Lower Grosvenor Place, London SW1W 0EY

Caravan Club, East Grinstead House, East Grinstead, W. Sussex

Europ Assistance, 269-273 High Street, Croydon Surrey, CR0 1QH

RAC, RAC House, Lansdowne Road, Croydon Surrey, CR9 2JA

Youth Hostels Association (England and Wales), 14 Southampton Street, London WC2

Scottish Youth Hostels Association, 7 Glebe Crescent, Stirling

Customs and Excise, Atlantic House, Holborn Viaduct, London EC1

In USA Portuguese National Tourist Office, 548 Fifth Avenue, NYC 10036: Palmer House (Suite 500), 17 East Monroe Street, Chicago, IL 60603: 1 Park Plaza (Suite 1305), 3250 Wilshire Boulevard, Los Angeles, CA 90010.

Portuguese Embassy, 1875 Connecticut Avenue North West, Washington DC, 20008.

TAP Portuguese Airlines, 1140 Avenue of the Americas, NYC 10036
Britrail, 270 Madison Avenue, NYC 10016
French National Railroads, 610 Fifth Avenue, NYC 10020
CIEE, 777 United Nations Plaza, NYC 10017
Consumers' Union, Mt Vernon, NY 10550
IAMAT, 350 Fifth Avenue (Suite 5620), NYC 10001
World Medical Association, 1841 Broadway, NYC 10023
American Youth Hostels Association, 132 Spring Street, NYC 10012
US Customs Service, Department of the Treasury, Washington,
    DC 20229

In Canada Portuguese National Tourist Office, 390 Bay Street,
    Toronto, Ont M5H 2Y2
Portuguese Embassy, 645 Ireland Park Road, Ottawa, Ontario
TAP Portuguese Airlines, 800 Dorchester Boulevard West,
    Montreal
Britrail, 55 Eglinton Avenue East, Toronto 12, Ont M4P 1G8:
    United Kingdom Building (Suite 1102), 409 Granville Street,
    Vancouver 2, V6C 1T2
French National Railroads, 1500 Stanley Street, Montreal,
    Quebec H3A 1R3; 409 Granville Street (Suite 452),
    Vancouver 2, BC V6C 1T2
Canadian Youth Hostels Association, 333 River Road, Vanier City,
    Ottawa
Voyageur Travel Insurance, 75 Selby Road, Brampton, Ont
    L6V 9Z9
Canada Customs have offices in Halifax, Quebec, Montreal,
    Ottawa, Toronto, Hamilton, London, Windsor, Winnipeg,
    Regina, Calgary, Vancouver: see telephone directories

In Portugal British Embassy, Rua São Domingo à Lapa 37,
    Lisbon
Canadian Embassy, Rua Rosa Araújo 2-62, Lisbon
US Embassy, Avenida Duque de Loulé 39, Lisbon
Air Canada (c/o TAP), 79 Rua Conde de la Redondo, Lisbon
British Airways, Avenida da Liberdade 23-27, Lisbon
British Caledonian, c/o Pan Am, below
CP Air, Avenida da Liberdade 261, Lisbon
Pan Am, Praça dos Restauradores 46, Lisbon
TWA, Avenida da Liberdade 258A, Lisbon
Portuguese Youth Hostels Association (Associacão de Pousadas
de Juventude), Avenida Duque de Avila 137, Lisbon

Prices

All figures quoted must be treated as approximate. Changes are too rapid nowadays for any publication to be certain of accuracy.

Exchange rates (Spring 1979) £1 = 100$00: US$1 = 48$75: CA$1 = 41$65. 1$00 = 1p = US¢2 = CA¢2½.

General Prices in general are below the UK's and North America's. Handicraft items, fashion wear, and things you may buy as presents or souvenirs are usually very good value. If you go food-shopping you will find home-produced wine, vegetables, fruit, olive oil, sugar, and rice very cheap indeed, and butter (when available) cheap.

Air travel
From UK London-Lisbon return: 1st-class £286, economy £188, excursion £141, advance booking £70-96 (Faro £76-103), London-Oporto £67.50-£91.00, minimum-rated packages (Lisbon and Faro) from £60.

From USA New York-Lisbon roundtrip: 1st-class US$1100, economy $616, excursion from $424, GITs from $300, APEX from $300, ABC from $300, charters from $320.

From Canada Montreal-Lisbon roundtrip: 1st-class CA$1420, economy $736, excursion $469-576, GITs $366-557, APEX $392-558.

In Portugal Lisbon-Faro one-way 1000$.

Rail travel
From UK London-Lisbon: 2nd-class single £56.65.

Rail bargains InterRail £97, Eurailpass US$190 for 15 days, Eurail Youthpass US$60.

In Portugal Lisbon-Faro one-way 255$.

Bus in Portugal Long-distance: as 2nd-class rail. Towns: 4-18$00.

Taxi Hiring 10$00 + 5$00 per 200m.

Ferries Across Tagus: 7$50.

Car hire Self-drive: 340-1500$00 + 3$40-11$50 per km.

Hotels Double with bath per night: 5-star from 1280-3350$00 (provinces) to 3700-3900$ (Algarve: Lisbon midway), 4-star 1250-2000$, 3-star 900$00-1400$, 2-star 700-1100$00, 1-star 500-900$. *Pousadas* 500-900$00, *estalagens* 470-1400$, *pensões*, 250-900$.

Restaurant meals 1st-class from 450$00, 2nd-class from 350$00, simple from 200$00, cafeteria from 150$00, *tascas* etc cheaper.

Bar drinks and snacks Coffee 5$00, tea 15$00, orange juice 15$00, beer 8$00, 1 litre carafe wine 45$00, bottle of wine 70$00, glass of port or madeira 20$00, whisky (large) 60$00, hamburger 25$00, sandwiches 13$00, ice cream 10$00.

Entertainments Fado restaurant meal from 250$00, disco or night-club from 450$00, bullfight 80-700$00, concerts 40-250$00.

Museum admission 2$50-10$00. Zoo 25$00.

Telephone Local call (3 mins) 2$50.

Motoring Petrol: 31$ per litre, normal 28$. Car wash (automatic) 60$. Parking 3$50-10$ per hour, 50-130$ per day. Tolls: 25 April Bridge 25$, motorways 17$50-30$. Campsites: allow about 150$ for car + tent + two adults on good site.

Motoring, camping and caravanning

Driving in Portugal is pleasant. Apart from short stretches of motorway and some new highways, roads are admittedly neither wide nor fast, and a few stretches are bumpy and cobbled. But except in big-city rush hours traffic is decidedly light—a very welcome change. However, it brings a minor problem of its own: like all drivers on empty roads (including you and me) the Portuguese may become careless. But they are not aggressive, and their driving is a good deal less frightening than in many countries.

A major point to keep in mind is that, apart from a few relatively busy roads near Lisbon and the main road north to Oporto, nearly all Portugal's roads are mountain roads. After coming over a high range you often think you are coming to level ground. But you are not: you simply twist and turn at a lower level.

Documents and insurance To take your car into Portugal for up to 1 year you need the registration book (log book) and your driving licence—not a provisional one, of course. If the car is not registered in your name you must have a letter of authority from the registered owner certified by a recognised motoring organisation such as, in UK, the AA or RAC and, in America, a state automobile club affiliated to the AAA or similar national body. If you cannot take the log book (if the car is hired, for instance), a complicated certi-fication is needed which any AIT-affiliated motoring organisation (AA, RAC, AAA, CAA, etc) will see to for members. Third-party insurance is not compulsory, but it is obviously advisable, if your car is insured in Europe, to have a 'green-card'—a document certifying that your insurance cover has been extended to Portugal and other countries you may be driving through. You obtain this for a usually small sum (charges vary) from your own insurance company. Apply in good time.

To drive en route through Spain you need also an international driving permit, obtainable in UK from the AA or RAC and in North America from the AAA or CAA, and a 'bail bond' from your insurers. The latter saves you being jailed and your car impounded pending the settlement of any court action or legal claim against you, following an accident in Spain. The bail bond is issued automatically and without charge along with the green card, if you tell your insurance company you are visiting Spain.

Additional Insurance The green card extends European residents' insurance to other European countries. It does not cover extra costs that may occur after accidents or breakdowns, such as flying out spare parts, paying for additional hotels, or for air tickets home, and so on. Such risks are covered by policies issued by insurance companies, the motoring organisations, the Caravan Club, etc. Europ Assistance do it cheaply and well.

Laws In Portugal you drive on the right and overtake on the left.

Priority Apart from the motorway near Lisbon and on clearly marked priority roads you give way to all traffic coming from your right (unless from a private drive). Remember that you will often have priority over vehicles on your left.

Headlights Right-hand drive UK cars should have their headlights modified. It is a nuisance for everyone, including yourself, if they dip left instead of right. The easiest way of altering them is to buy a set of lenses from a garage, car accessory shop, the AA or RAC, etc. Since from UK and elsewhere you have to drive through Spain carry a full set of spare lamps to save a possible on-the-spot fine for not having all your compulsory lamps in working order.

Speed limits in built-up areas are 60 km p h (37 mph) for cars without trailers and 50 km p h (31 mph) with trailers. Outside towns 90 km p h (55 mph) on main roads, 70 km p h (43 mph) with trailers, and 120 km p h (75 mph) on motorways, are the respective speed limits.

Parking restrictions are precise. You must not park on a bridge, within 5 m of a bend or tram stop, within 10 m of a bus stop, in front of a driveway or entrance to a public park, school, church or theatre, on the brow of a hill, or within 30 m of a road junction or crossroads. Nor, of course, where there are 'No Parking' signs. Parking discs, obtainable free from police stations and some tourist information offices, must be used in Lisbon and other towns with a 'blue zone' (*Zona azul*).

Warning triangles are compulsory in Portugal. They must be placed 30 m (35 yards) behind the car and visible from 100 m—unless the stopped car is itself visible from 100 m.

Use of the horn is forbidden in all built-up areas—and the ban is respected. On the open road it is not compulsory to sound your horn before overtaking, as it is in some countries, but it is not a bad idea.

Carry your documents As in most European countries, you are legally obliged to carry your car documents, driving licence, and personal identity documents with you at all times. Police operate quite frequent spot checks and you must, of course, produce insurance certificate, driving licence, and passport if involved in an accident.

Fines Remember that on-the-spot fines can be imposed by the police for most straightforward traffic offences, such as wrong parking, exceeding the speed limit, etc.

Drink Penalties for driving under the influence of drink or drugs are particularly severe.

Roads, signposting, garages, tolls
Road standards are sound, though not outstanding. Sections paved with basalt setts should be treated with very great caution after light rain, when they become terrifyingly slippery. When completely dry they are safe, but noisy and therefore tiring.

Road signs in general follow the Continental pattern. One Portuguese speciality however is the use of speed limit signs by themselves to warn you of obstructions ahead, such as narrow bridges or ramps. If you meet a 50 km, and then a 30 km sign just before a blind corner, take them seriously. Roads are numbered and the numbers prefixed with N (for *nacional*). You are not likely to drive on non-national roads unless visiting very out-of-the-way places.

Directional signposting is fairly good on major roads. The next main town and the road number are normally clearly posted at exits from towns. Rather oddly, however, the main destination often is not repeated at turnings off the main road. On side roads, signposting often peters out after you have left the major route. Signs vanish in towns. The Michelin 37 map (Portugal) is essential for serious motoring. Accurate maps of the Algarve region are unfortunately non-existent.

Petrol stations and garages are plentiful enough on main roads, and often stay open till very late. Manufacturers' accredited agents for most widely-used makes of car can be found in Lisbon, Oporto, and some other towns. Repairs are usually carefully done and, again, repair stations are often open late on Monday to Friday. UK residents may however consider it worth while to hire a spare parts pack through a garage or the AA or RAC, who will also advise on what to take.

Tolls are payable on short lengths of motorway near Lisbon, on the 25 April Bridge over Tagus in Lisbon, and of course on the Tagus ferries. Charges are very low.

Breakdowns and accidents If you break down, you have to get help from a nearby service station. Fellow motorists will often help.

Accidents In general take action as at home. Have the police called if anyone is injured. Above all, try to get names and addresses of witnesses. After an accident provide your name and address by showing your driving licence (also your passport) and allow any interested person to copy your insurance company's name and address from your insurance certificate.

Ambulances and crews are stationed at roughly 30 km intervals along the busiest roads. They, and the police, can be called from 'SOS Call' telephones provided every 3-4 km. Dial 115.

Road Distance Chart: distances in km by main through roads

| Town | From | | |
	Lisbon	Oporto	Faro
Aveiro	275	78	581
Beja	189	388	154
Braga	365	50	671
Bragança	544	251	850
Castelo Branco	268	271	329
Coimbra	199	116	502
Elvas	222	506	394
Estoril	27	350	330
Évora	142	457	205
Faro	304	619	—
Guarda	365	223	488
Lisbon	—	315	304
Nazaré	118	230	422
Oporto	315	—	619
Portalegre	233	360	306
Santarém	77	225	285
Sintra	28	320	334
Viana do Castelo	385	70	789
Viseu	277	138	469

Getting there

From UK Calais, Boulogne, Le Touquet, Dieppe, Le Havre, and
Cherbourg are the best ports to make for. They are served by
Sealink, Townsend-Thoresen, Seaspeed, Hoverlloyd, and
Normandy Ferries. Harwich-Ostend may also be a suitable route
if you are starting from East Anglia, the Midlands, or further north.

The key point to head for in France is Bordeaux. From Ostend,
Calais, Boulogne, or Le Touquet join the northern (A1) motorway
to Paris. Circle the city anti-clockwise by the dual-carriageway
Boulevard périphérique and leave by the A13/A12/N10 for Chartres,
Bordeaux, and Biarritz to the Spanish frontier at Hendaye-Irún.
From Dieppe and Le Havre join either the A13 at Rouen or the
N10 at Chartres or Tours. From Cherbourg head for Angers and
the N10 at Poitiers. A good and up-to-date map of France is
essential because of current new road construction. The Michelin
No. 989 is probably the best.

An easy route inside Spain is via Burgos (N1), Valladolid,
Salamanca, and Fuentes de Onoro (N620). From Salamanca you can
alternatively continue south to Cáceres (N630), and turn west on
the N521 for Lisbon (N16 inside Portugal); or to Mérida (still
N630) where you turn west on the NV (N4 inside Portugal) to
Lisbon. Yet another possibility is to drive via Madrid (N1) Córdoba
and Seville (NIV), and Ayamonte (N431), where you cross the
River Guadiana by ferry direct to the Algarve coast. Main-road
frontier posts are open 07.00-24.00 (and sometimes 01.00) in
summer, and 08.00-21.00 (sometimes 24.00) in winter.

Short cuts and leisurely runs You can cut down driving by taking
Brittany Ferries' Plymouth-Santander service (approx 24 hours).
From Santander (on Spain's northern coast) you can travel south
to Burgos, and then as above. Or you can cross the high Pajares
Pass south of Oviedo and continue through León and Zamora.

Car-sleeper trains from Boulogne, Dieppe, Rouen, and Paris to
Biarritz (all in France) also shorten your journey. Other useful
car-sleepers link Paris or Irún and Madrid, and Madrid and Lisbon.
Most operate only on certain days from April to October.
Information can be obtained in UK from BR Travel Centres,
French Railways, or the Spanish National Tourist Office; and in
North America from Britrail or French National Railroad offices.

For a leisurely run try taking the strenuous and slow but very
attractive Spanish coast road (N634, etc) past Oviedo to Corunna
(La Coruña in Spanish), where you turn south through Santiago
de Compostela and Vigo (N550) and enter Portugal at Valença do
Minho.

Picturesque roads Almost everywhere you drive in Portugal you will find yourself giving exclamations of delight every few minutes— the only exceptions to the beautiful scenery being some of the areas round Lisbon, Oporto, much of the Estremandura province, and parts of the Algarve—and even here the towns and villages are lovely. The Michelin map of Portugal (No. 37) prints a green border to all roads considered picturesque—and there is more green border on the Michelin 37 than on any other map in the series. Even where green is scarce, notably in the vast Alentejo province, you will find the scenery very attractive and the villages extraordinarily colourful. Three really outstanding drives are outlined in our What to See section under Douro Valley, Serra da Estrela, and Sintra.

Camping and Caravanning
Portugal's climate provides a long season during which camping and caravanning is thoroughly enjoyable. If you wish, you can camp or park your 'van, with the owner's permission, on any land that is not inside a built-up area, in a protected water-supply zone, on a beach or other public open space, or within 1 km (just over $\frac{1}{2}$ mile) from an organised campsite. Well equipped sites, however, are available in many spots of general tourist interest. They are more frequent in the north. But there are enough everywhere to enable car-campers and caravanners to see and enjoy every part of the country. A list giving details of available facilities can be obtained free from the Portuguese National Tourist Office. All sites accept trailer and motor caravans. Prices are extremely reasonable.

Camping carnets and memberships of camping or caravanning clubs are not essential. They are however advisable as they provide third-party insurance for damage you may do to other people's property, and serve also as introductions to sites owned and run by local clubs and other private bodies, such as the Portuguese Camping and Caravanning Federation (Federação Portuguesa de Campismo e Caravanismo). You obtain carnets from camping and caravanning clubs, motoring associations etc. An organisation called Orbitur runs about 15 of the better sites. Many others belong to local authorities or local tourist associations. Campsites are called *parques de campismo* in Portuguese.

Caravans Trailer-caravanners intending to tour Portugal would be well advised to study the map before leaving so as to avoid too much towing on narrow, uneven, and often steep mountain roads. If you are keeping to coastal regions, few problems arise. But if you want to explore the interior, choose a limited number of bases reachable by the wider and less winding roads, and make day excursions from them. The Michelin 37 shows road widths and indicates pretty clearly which roads are packed tight with bends.

Azulejos decoration at the University Chapel of Coimbra (p. 33)

Life Portuguese Style

The Portuguese are strongly Catholic, extremely conservative in their habits and outlook, but delightfully hospitable to friendly strangers. Strongly rooted in their own localities, they remain almost fiercely loyal to local traditions and celebrate local festivals with an enthusiasm that has not waned over the centuries. Despite the publicity efforts of the official tourist organisations, these religious processions and fairs have not become, by any means, mere tourist shows. In fact, you will find relatively few foreigners present at most of them. Portugal, however, is not a country that has been left behind in the past. It is thoroughly modern and, at the same time, a place where a traditional way of life still lasts.

In the realm of art there is a wealth of lovely and often unusual items produced by Portugal's artists—outstanding amongst them the painters Cristóvão de Figueiredo, Garcia Fernandes, and Gregório Lopes; and the sculptors Nicolas Chanterene and Houdant. But despite this, many people will feel that the country's art really belongs to the thousands of unnamed craftsmen who still produce the great variety of magnificent ceramics to be found in many regions, the fine lace and handwoven rugs, carpets, bedspreads and blankets, gold and silver filigree work, superbly carved woodwork, and simple—or not so simple—baskets. Portugal is a country where the annual fairs and even the weekly markets are a joy to attend because of the beauty and variety and reasonable price of the goods on sale. Even the decorations that ordinary fishermen paint on their boats are something decidedly out of the ordinary—as every visitor soon discovers.

Music, like art, belongs in Portugal as much to the people as to specialist composers and performers. Radio and television have made inroads, but in every province the old traditional dances are still performed to the same music and with the same songs as in centuries past. In the Algarve it is the lively *corridinho,* in Alentejo mournful *saias* and *balhas,* in Ribatejo stately *fandangos* and *escovinhos,* in Minho and Douro rhythmic and energetic *viras* and *gotas,* and so on throughout the country. Displays of folk-dance and music are organised now in tourist centres. In addition, many places have festivals of ordinary orchestral and other music.

Though commonly regarded abroad as a national tradition, the *fado* really belongs only to Lisbon and to Coimbra. It is a rather mournful song, often sung by a woman, about fate or some similarly serious topic. Accompanied by twelve-stringed Portuguese guitars with a six-stringed Spanish guitar as background, it is sung in special restaurants in Lisbon by professional *fadistas,* and in Coimbra by students. No one knows the fado's origin. It appears to have emerged in Portugal towards the end of the 18th century, possibly influenced by sailors' songs. But it is always taken very seriously—by audiences as well as performers. If you visit one of the Lisbon fado restaurants do not treat it as you might other mealtime music, and chatter happily through it: you will be thoroughly unwelcome if you do. Fado singing starts late and may last till dawn; do not arrive before 23.00. There are also a lot of amateur fado clubs.

History

Portugal's early history corresponds to that of all the western Mediterranean region. First came the establishment of Phoenician and Greek coastal trading posts (from the 9th and 6th centuries BC respectively), then involvement in Rome's Phoenician (or 'Punic') wars against Carthage in the 3rd and 2nd centuries, and finally conquest by Rome and incorporation into the prosperous Roman Empire. The country's modern history begins with Rome's collapse and the Visigoth invasion of the 5th century AD.

Portugal's present 9 million inhabitants are descended very largely from the Lusitanian tribes who were there when the Phoenicians first arrived, from the Romans who settled there for nearly 700 years, and from invading Visigoth tribes. The close-packed mountain ranges which make up most of Portugal—not high, but a barrier to easy communications—and the sea, have kept Portugal largely isolated till modern times, even from her Spanish neighbours. The country has developed on distinctive lines.

In AD 711 a 'Moorish' army made up of Arabs and Islamised

Berbers invaded Spain and Portugal from North Africa, and overran almost the whole Iberian Peninsula. It was from the Asturias, a part of north-west Spain not effectively conquered by the Moors, that the reconquest of Portugal began. It started early —much earlier than in Spain. By the 9th century the county of 'Portucale' (from the Latin *Portus Cale*, see p. 64) was in Christian hands, and the country still called 'Portugal' had begun its existence. By 1147 its boundaries had been extended south to Lisbon. In 1249 the extreme southern province of the Algarve (Arabic *al-Gharb* means 'the west') was recaptured and the last Moors expelled.

The foundation of a university in Lisbon in 1290 (moved to Coimbra in 1308), with teachers drawn from Bologna, Oxford, Salamanca, Paris, and elsewhere, made Portugal one of Europe's most famous centres of learning.

A little over a century later, the capture of Ceuta, some 64 km east of Tangier on Morocco's Mediterranean coast, began a century of expansion and exploration in which Portugal's seamen led the world and discovered much that no Europeans had previously seen. The purpose of Ceuta's capture was to make Moorish raids on Portuguese shipping more difficult. The real mainspring of Portuguese exploration, however, was the scientific advances in shipbuilding, map-making, and navigation that resulted from the school of navigation established by Prince Henry the Navigator on the windswept, flat clifftop looking across to Cape St Vincent, near Sagres. It is an inspiring spot, which you can still visit.

Improved navigational instruments were developed here, making it possible to fix positions exactly by the stars for the first time. Far better charts than other nations possessed were drawn. A new type of sea-going vessel, the caravel, was produced. Its shallow draught and stern rudder ensured manageability; its wide, enclosed hull provided more shelter than crews had been accustomed to; and its several masts, instead of just one, ensured a considerable spread of sail and greater speed as well as ability to tack against the wind.

Madeira was discovered in 1420, and the Azores in 1427. In 1434 a Portuguese ship sailed further down Africa's west coast than any modern European had previously been. The mouth of the River Congo was reached in 1482, and Brazil in 1500. Meanwhile Columbus, refused help in Portugal, had discovered the New World for the rulers of Spanish Castile in 1492.

Prince Henry had died in 1460 but his work went on. Bartolomeu Dias, reached Tempest Cape in 1488, renamed Cape of Good Hope by the Portuguese King. Ten years later Vasco da Gama had reached Mozambique and India. By 1540 commercial relations were being established with China, Siam, and Indonesia. The Portuguese route to the orient was protected by a number of fortified posts. Portugal had not only achieved a monopoly of the Far Eastern trade, previously run by Turks and Arabs, but she had also diverted much of the trade that previously passed through Mediterranean ports such as Venice and Genoa, or through the Baltic ports, to her own harbours, mainly Lisbon. Spain, with vast colonial possessions in the New World, was her great rival.

For a tiny country this was a fantastic achievement. But it turned out an exhausting one. Wealth poured into the country, but people and skills flowed out. The population decreased from 2 million to 1 million; the land stopped being properly cultivated; craftsmen went elsewhere; and much newly-won wealth was dissipated in paying for imports. An attempt to lead a sort of Crusade against Moslem North Africa—part of its object was to find the fabled Christian kingdom, beyond the Moslem lands, ruled by the legendary Prester John, and to exploit its presumed wealth—ended Portugal's power and also its independence.

Philip II of Spain invaded and conquered the country in 1580 and had himself crowned Philip I of Portugal. But the Portuguese were never content to be ruled by Spain. In 1640 the Duke of Braganza rebelled, and assumed the title of King John IV of Portugal. The marriage of his daughter Catherine to Charles II of England in 1662 was an indication of Portuguese-British understanding: it, incidentally, gave Tangier and Bombay, part of her dowry, to Britain. In 1668 Spain recognised Portugal's independence. The dynasty established by John of Braganza continued to rule Portugal till 1910. John himself was descended from the earlier line of Portuguese kings begun in 1386 by João I and his Queen, Philippa, daughter of England's John of Gaunt.

In 1703 England and Portugal signed a commercial treaty, the Methuen Treaty, by which British woollens were exchanged for Portuguese port wine. In 1755 a terrible earthquake devastated Lisbon (see p. 44) causing a huge amount of damage elsewhere.

By the turn of the century Portugal and Britain were jointly facing revolutionary France. In 1808 British troops under Wellington landed in Portugal to help expel the French invaders. Six years later, after a series of brilliant but very hard campaigns, Portugal was again free. But war's impoverishment brought discontent, intrigue, and civil war, which lasted till 1834. Meanwhile Brazil, Portugal's richest possession, had become independent in 1828.

Discontent continued in various forms through the 19th century and culminated with the assassination of both the king and the heir to the throne in 1908. The Republic declared in 1910 was however unable to achieve stability, though it sent a force to help the Allies against Germany in 1916.

A critical economic situation in the late 1920s and early 1930s led to a seizure of power in 1932 by Dr Oliveira Salazar, who had been Minister of Finance since 1928. As President from 1932 to his retirement in 1968, Dr Salazar ruled Portugal with a very firm hand. The dictatorial form of government he established formally in 1933 survived until 25 April 1974 when it collapsed under a sudden upsurge of popular feeling, led by the army. The country held its first free parliamentary election for nearly half a century in 1975. The years following have not been easy.

Portugal today, despite modern developments, is still a mainly agricultural country. Some 30% of the working population is engaged in farming. Cereals, vines, olives, fruit and vegetables, cattle and other stock, and timber—especially cork, for Portugal can claim one-third of all the world's cork oaks—are the main products. But the land is not fertile. The sea still supplements the nation's income and its food resources. Over 30,000 men are engaged in fishing and ten times as much fish as meat is eaten in Lisbon. Portugal's merchant navy transports much of her overseas trade, including that with present and former overseas territories such as, respectively, the Azores and Mozambique.

Mining occupies an important place in the industrial field. It produces iron ore, uranium, tungsten, tin, and other metals, together with marble, granite, and slate. Many mineral resources, however, are still not being exploited. Manufacturing industries include oil refining, ironworks, fertiliser factories, car assembly plants, wiremills, cotton and wool weaving mills, cork-making plants, and canneries for fish and other products. Industrial development is linked to the increased supply of hydro-electric power. Over 30 dams have been built in 30 years and capacity is expected to double within the next 10. A quarter of the country's total population already lives in the industrialised areas around Lisbon and Oporto. But despite growing industrialisation and an inevitable drift to the towns, as well as the increased importance of tourism, Portugal remains a delightfully 'unspoilt' country.

Architecture

Specifically Portuguese styles began to emerge even before the country became independent. Romanesque churches were built in granite in northern regions during the 11th and 12th centuries. Cathedrals of this style and date were constructed to be as much fortresses as places of worship: the one at Coimbra is a notable example. Portuguese Gothic flourished during the 13th and 14th centuries, especially in the area near Lisbon: the churches and monasteries to be seen at Santarém, Alcobaça, and Batalha are outstanding examples. As Gothic began to merge into Renaissance, Portugal developed the most distinctive of all its architectural styles, called Manueline because it flourished in the reign of Manuel I (1490-1520). It was magnificently imaginative and decorative, using everything from flowers, leaves, corncobs, and even artichokes to anchors, globes, and ropes as models for its sculpture. The most famous example is the window designed by Diogo de Arruda in the Convent of Christ at Tomar. In the 16th century, too, Spanish Plateresque style—exceptionally rich reliefs carved in the manner of silversmiths' work (Spanish *platero* means silversmith)—appeared in Portugal. In the same way, in earlier years, there had been examples of what are called by the Spanish names Mudejar and Mozarabic styles. The first is applied to Christian buildings in which Moorish influence can be traced, and the second to the work of Christian craftsmen done for Moorish masters or under Moorish inspiration. During the Manueline period a new development along these lines was the 'Luso-Moorish' style evolved by Francisco de Arruda, brother of the Tomar window designer.

Though Portugal's prosperity and independence disappeared before the end of the 16th century, architecture continued to flourish through the Classical and Baroque periods of the 17th and 18th centuries. Fine examples of baroque can be seen in Lisbon, Oporto, Braga, Mafra, and elsewhere.

Apart from the many examples of religious architecture, Portugal's castles deserve special study. The earliest, such as the one which crowns the lovely northern walled town of Bragança and those at Guimarães, and Leiria, were built to establish control over territory reconquered from the Moors. Those built or rebuilt from the 13th to 17th century guarded main roads: the ones at Estremoz, Evoramonte, and elsewhere are good examples. Finally a number were built or rebuilt at places such as Elvas, in the 17th century, to defend the frontier with Spain.

Windmills and watermills survive in many places, and the traditional house-building styles of every region that are one of Portugal's most fascinating and attractive features, varying from the low, whitewashed, almost windowless cottages of the southern Alentejo province, with their huge chimneys, to the small granite-built Minho homes where broad staircases lead up to first-floor verandas large enough to be used as open-air sitting rooms. Elegant small Moorish-style chimneys are a distinctive feature of the Algarve's small white houses.

Rather surprisingly, beautifully designed old pillories are frequent. These were erected in every place which had the right to hold courts and administer justice. They consist of a single column, to which the cage containing a criminal was attached in bygone days, often topped by a decoration based on the cage theme.

Around the middle of the 14th century Portugal began to manufacture *azulejos*—decorative tiles, at first in geometric patterns, based on a blue (*azul*) background. Moorish tiles had been 'discovered' when Ceuta was captured in 1415, and imported from Morocco, or the Moorish province of Andalusia in southern Spain, for 150 years. But after about 1580 Portugal manufactured her own and a positive craze for them lasted until the end of the 18th century: you see the results all over the country. Geometric patterns were soon abandoned in favour of elaborate and beautiful pictures covering large areas of wall. At the beginning of the craze many tiles were imported from Delft and other Dutch sources.

Traditional Festivals

Portugal's traditional local festivals are very numerous and occur throughout the year. They can be divided into two main categories —*feiras*, or fairs, probably originally connected with seasonal tasks in agriculture or other occupations; and *romarias* (the word means literally 'journeys to Rome'), which are more directly religious in origin and usually include religious processions and pilgrimages to sacred shrines. These are always colourful, with brightly coloured traditional clothes, statues of saints, candles, and often musicians, including a *gaitero* or bagpiper (the instrument is less powerful than the Scottish pipes) and a tambourine player. Fireworks may be let off when the procession reaches the shrine. Each locality has its own traditions.

Once the religious celebration is completed, secular festivities begin. Folk-dancing, fireworks, music, stalls selling local handicrafts, and sometimes a sort of gigantic mass picnic are the form the festivities usually take. Many *feiras* and *romarias* last more than one day. Perhaps their most attractive feature is the fact that they are still very much a product of local life, intended for the local people's edification and entertainment. Only those at Viana do Castelo and Fátima have achieved much international fame, and even here you will find relatively few foreign visitors. In Lisbon festivals include mass marriages at the Cathedral on 13 June.

Bullfighting may form part of the celebrations at certain fairs. But it is really a separate traditional sport, practised from Easter to October. The Portuguese version has developed very differently from Spain's. Since the 18th century it has been forbidden to kill a bull in the ring: the object is to master and immobilise it.

The bullfight (*tourada*) opens with a spectacular procession of all the participants. Then the horsemen (*cavaleiros*) provoke the bull by their riding, and at the same time wear it down with darts (*farpas*, the equivalent of the Spanish *banderillas*) stuck into fleshy muscles. At a suitable moment the final stage (*pega*) begins. The horsemen give way to eight *moços de forcado* on foot. Their leader's job is, first, to demonstrate his skill by jumping over the bull's horns, then to seize the animal by the horns while the others help immobilise it. If this proves impossible, he has to seize its withers from the side while the others pull on the animal's tail and so prevent it from moving. The bull is usually slaughtered in the normal way the following day.

The best fighting bulls are bred in the Ribatejo province, and the best bullfights take place in Lisbon, Santarém, and Vila Franca de Xira.

Sport

Portugal is much better provided with sports facilities than most people realise. Espinho and Estoril, for instance, have had 18-hole golf courses of good quality for many years. Newer and even more lavish 18-hole courses have been built in more recent years near Caparica, at Penina (designed and managed by Henry Cotton), Monte Gordo, Vale de Lobo, Quinta do Lago and Vilamoura on the Algarve coast. Additional 9-hole courses exist at Praia de Granja (near Espinho), Vidago (inland north-east), and Praia de Porto Novo (south of Peniche). Tennis courts too, are available in most sizeable towns and resorts.

Deep-sea angling, spear fishing, and scuba diving are of an equally high standard. Virtually every sizeable coast resort can provide facilities for sea fishing, though the types of catch vary. From the extreme north to the Tagus estuary, bass, grey bream, grey and red mullet, eels, sole, and pout whiting are the main fish caught. From Sesimbra southwards and all along the Algarve coast big-game and deep-sea catches include swordfish, tunny, and various types of shark. Troll-fishing produces bass, coalfish, bluefish, bream, and other varieties. Tope, bonito, mullet, conger and moray eels, and much else can be caught inshore. The Hotel Espadarte at Sesimbra, and the Batador restaurant at Sagres (near the Hotel de Baleeira) cater specially for deep-sea anglers, though boats and equipment can be hired at most larger resorts.

Neither sea fishing nor spear fishing requires a permit. Both can be practised throughout the year. Areas specially recommended for spear fishing are: Peniche, Berlenga Island, Sesimbra, Sines, and—best of all—Sagres. Visibility off Sesimbra can be poor in winter, and off Peniche occasional cloudiness occurs. Conditions otherwise are normally good. Underwater life is particularly rich and plentiful at the Algarve coast's western end.

Scuba diving is similarly free of restrictions, though you should ask locally about areas that may be forbidden for security or other reasons. Clear waters, rocky headlands and coves, and the tremendous variety of marine life make it very attractive. Aqualung clubs exist in many towns and resorts. Air-bottles can be refilled in Lisbon, Oporto, and the Algarve.

Sailing and water-skiing are as yet relatively little developed. Only the biggest resorts, such as Cascais, Albufeira, Faro, and Praia da Rocha, have well-established arrangements for water-skiing; one obvious reason is the fact that the Atlantic which washes Portugal's shores is not the smoothest of oceans. And while every sizeable harbour can find moorings for visiting yachts, Portugal's first modern-style yacht marina has only recently been built at Vilamoura on the Algarve coast. Further developments will certainly be on the way.

Portugal's lakes and rivers throughout the country offer good fishing for trout, barbel, carp, club and other species—also salmon in some areas. Sea trout and brown trout can be caught in northern rivers such as the Minho and Lima. Permits are not required on Sundays or public holidays, nor by foreign visitors. If you do buy one (from the local town hall), the cost is negligible. Fishing is, however, legally forbidden during the hours of darkness, and there are closed seasons for salmon and trout (August 1st to end of February) and for all other species (March 15th-July 31st).

Riding is very popular, particularly in resorts and holiday areas, and there is no shortage of horses for hire. Centres have been developed mainly in the newer resorts and the bigger towns such as Leiria, Oporto, and of course Lisbon. But they are spreading to smaller places too.

Among less widely practised sports a certain amount of mainly rough shooting is possible. An import permit for shotguns and up to 400 cartridges must be obtained from the Customs on arrival, and a game licence obtained after payment of a 1000$ deposit against the guns' re-export. Winter skiing is possible in the Serra da Estrela. Roller skating is surprisingly popular among the Portuguese. Rinks can be found in most sizeable towns.

Entertainment

For evening entertainment Portugal can provide standard-type discothèques, mainly in the Cascais-Estoril region and in the chief international resorts. In these and other places, especially Lisbon, you will also find what are called *boîtes* and *nightclubs*. Boîte is, of course, the French word for nightclub. In Portuguese, however, it often indicates what in France is known—with the aid of an equally misused English word—as *un dancing*—a bar where you can dance. The term nightclub is applied mostly to places where you can dine and enjoy a floorshow as well as dance. Distinctions between the different types of nightspot are, however, becoming blurred. Some discothèques and boîtes also serve dinner.

In Estoril the smartest nightclub is in the Casino, which also offers gambling. Other casinos exist at Espinho, Figueira da Foz, Cascais, Póvoa de Varzim, and Vila do Conde. The Algarve's first Casino opened at Penina in 1973, followed by another at Vilamoura, and a third at Monte Gordo, all under the same management. All have nightclubs, bars, and restaurants as well as gambling. Visitors are legally obliged to show passports when entering a casino.

Apart from the 'fado restaurants' in Lisbon (p. 30), there are plenty of bars in every corner of the country where men can, and do, go to enjoy themselves. Respectable females, however, do not go into most bars, not even with their menfolk, unless they are foreign visitors inside an international tourist precinct. Women's special preserve, in Lisbon and other big towns, is the *tearooms* where they gather for a 'five o'clock', tea (or coffee) and cream cakes.

Most towns and resorts have cinemas, open seven days a week, where mostly British and American films are run in English with Portuguese sub-titles. Lisbon, Oporto, and quite a number of other towns have theatres. In addition, there are the folklore displays and the concerts, given during music festivals in the larger centres, already mentioned (p. 35).

Bullfighting apart, soccer is easily the most popular spectator sport, with grounds in most large towns. Vila Real has a well-established motor-racing circuit and another opened recently at Estoril.

Food

Portuguese cooking is best described by the French term *paysan*, in the real meaning of 'belonging to the country'. The ingredients are fresh, not imported or frozen. They appear on the table when they are in season. They are plentiful and tasty, and the dishes made with them are filling. The richness extends to the sauces and seasonings, usually extremely spicy. Yet at the same time there is little that is likely to upset stomachs accustomed to less exuberant delights.

Soups are varied and unusual. *Caldo verde*, strictly belonging to the Minho province and made with mashed potatoes and finely chopped cabbage, has become a sort of national dish. Small slices of *tora*, a sort of black pudding, are added during cooking. But there are lots of other soups, including the *açordas*, made with bread. The Alentejo province's *sopa de coentros*, for example, floats a poached egg on a base of coriander, garlic, olive oil and bread, and is delicious. In the south a *gaspacho*, usually made with tomatoes, onions, cucumbers, pimentos, garlic, and vinegar, is served cold. Fish and shellfish soup (*sopa de peixe* and *sopa de mariscos*) is very popular. The term *caldeirada* is applied to both fish soup and fish stew. A *caldeirada a fragateira* resembles a southern French bouillabaisse, with a great mixture of ingredients.

Among fish dishes *bacalhau á gomes de sá* (stewed cod with, among other things, potatoes, eggs, and olives) is regarded as something of a national dish. But you will get fish and shellfish of every sort served in a large number of different ways. Fresh sardines are grilled over charcoal and served with potatoes and green peppers (*sardinhas assadas*). Lampreys (*lampreias*) and eels (*enguias*) are popular in the north. Crayfish (*lagostas*) may be served jugged, and giant prawns (*gambas*) baked. In the Algarve, oysters are cooked in a copper vessel with aromatic herbs and sausages.

Apart from pork (*porco*) and roast kid (*cabrito*), Portuguese meat is not in itself outstanding. But you will get many tasty casseroles and pot roasts. Pork is often smoked and served as cutlets (*paios*) or ham (*presunto*); sometimes smoked pig's tongue (*linguiça*), is eaten, or the pork mixed with oysters or mussels (*porco á Alentejana*). It is also added to other dishes, such as the *cozido á Portuguesa*, a beef hotpot with potatoes, vegetables, and rice. Other delicacies include tripe and roast sucking pig (*leitão assado*).

Vegetables are plentiful and varied in season. Spinach and asparagus are particularly good. Tomatoes are used in great quantity, especially in the excellent salads. Rice appears in innumerable guises, as both vegetable and dessert—it is in fact grown in parts of Portugal.

Among cheeses those made from ewes' milk, such as *queija de Castelo Branco* and *queija de Azeitão*, make specially good eating between May and October. The goats' milk cheeses—*cabreiro, robaçal,* and others—are also exceptionally tasty. If you are offered a local cheese, try it. More often than not you will get a very pleasant surprise.

Fruit is abundant, varied, and good as the vegetables. It includes raspberries, plums, melons, oranges, strawberries, peaches, and figs. But the Portuguese love to end a meal with dessert dishes whose lavish use of sugar betrays their oriental origin. Large numbers of towns and regions take pride in local dessert and pastry specialities. Torres Vedras's delicious *pasteis de feijão* are just one example—and not a well-known one either. Elsewhere you may be offered such things as *ovos moles*, a confection of egg yolks and sugar prepared in a shell-shaped mould.

Many other dishes also use eggs. The most popular way of serving rice, for instance, is known as *arroz doce*. The rice is first cooked with vanilla, lemon peel, and sugar. Then the vanilla pod and lemon peel are removed and egg yolks beaten in. The dish is served cold, sprinkled with cinnamon. Figs and almonds prevail, however, in Algarve desserts.

I must add one word of warning. Portuguese recipes have never been standardised to the extent that most French dishes have. Every cook has his (or her) own ideas, so that Portuguese cooking retains many of the delights—or drawbacks— of what French gastronomic writers call *cuisine impromptue*.

Drink

Portugal produces a considerable variety of table wines, many of which are not exported outside the producing region. If in doubt you can always ask for a *vinho da região* (local wine), which may be *tinto* (red), *branco* (white), or *rosé*. A straightforward, ordinary cheap wine is called *vinho de mesa* (table wine), often served in a jug or carafe.

The products of two wine regions, however, are particularly worth sampling—apart from port and Madeira, which demand separate discussion. These are the gently sparkling light-coloured white *vinhos verdes*, of low alcoholic content, from the Minho and lower Douro valley, and the red and white wines from the Dão valley. The *Colares* (red) and *Bucelas* (white) wines are also good. Many others also deserve to be better known, such as those from Ribatejo province, from Torres Vedras, Alcobaça, Chamusca, Agueda, and Lafões, and the Pinhel rosé. Mateus rosé needs no introduction.

Till very recent years, port was regarded—in Britain at least—as virtually a British drink, even though the after-dinner port-passing ritual of great houses, service messes, and Oxbridge senior common rooms is vanishing slowly into the past. But for some reason never fathomed, British port-drinkers take only the medium or sweet red port, the dessert wine, and neglect completely the dry or very dry white port which makes an excellent aperitif, much appreciated in Portugal and elsewhere.

Madeira comes from the island which has been a Portuguese possession for over 550 years. But what we call Madeira is usually the dessert wine known to the Portuguese as Boal. Like port, it

has also a dry, amber-coloured aperitif version, named Sercial.
The most famous dessert version, Malmsey, deep red and honey-
flavoured, is today difficult to find.

A number of brandies, liqueurs, and what the French call *alcools*
(similar to *framboise* and other drinks from eastern France) are
produced in Portugal, often on a strictly local basis. They are
worth sampling. Some are very acceptable.

When you are not drinking wine you will find that Portugal bottles
good spa waters. Luso is non-fizzy. Vidago, Pedras Salgadas,
Vimeiro and others—all from known spas—are fizzy in greater or
less degree. Various types of fruit juice are available, together with
soft drinks like Pepsi Cola and a local speciality, *capilé*, a sort of
sarsaparilla. Beers are of the light lager type. Coffee, including the
Portuguese-manufactured instant type, is usually very good. It is
served strong and black—except at breakfast—unless milk (*leite*) is
specifically asked for. Pasteurised milk is available only from
special shops, but litre bottles of sterilised milk, with a rather
different taste, can be bought everywhere.

What to see

If holidays for you mean lovely sandy beaches, good accommodation and plentiful evening entertainment, together with
things like riding, snorkelling, scuba diving, tennis, sea-fishing,
underwater fishing, and first-rate golf, Portugal can meet all your
needs. The two main sections of coast catering primarily for
foreign visitors are the long-established Costa do Sol (Sun Coast),
west of Lisbon, with Estoril and Cascais its main resorts, and the
fast-developing Algarve coast, where hotels were not built until
the early 1960s. Each of these regions has a distinctive character.
Even together, however, they contain only a fraction of Portugal's
total 850 km (530 miles) of sand. Inclusive-tour firms now include
a good selection of lesser-known but very attractive resorts.

Beaches and coast resorts, however, are only the start. Portugal
possesses an extraordinary and little-appreciated abundance of
old towns—places like Bragança, Evora, Estremoz, Lagos and
many others—and numerous magnificent medieval monasteries and
palaces. Its scenery, too, is outstanding. Most people do not realise
that Portugal is extremely mountainous. Though peaks are not
specially high, the mountain ranges are all but continuous. It
makes car touring, in particular, a constant delight.

Vegetation deserves a special note. Portugal is unique in presenting, in its tiny space, trees and shrubs and cultivated crops belonging to every sort of climate from North European to tropical
(see Sintra and Bussaco). The innumerable cultivated gardens are
naturally magnificent.

The country's different regions vary strikingly, even though tiny
Portugal would fit comfortably into a rectangle of only 600 km
(375 miles) by 240 km (150 miles). The variations are roughly
embodied in the ancient provinces' boundaries.

In the north the Minho province (modern administrative districts
of Viana do Castelo and Braga) is filled with tight-packed granite
hills, densely wooded, and its little-known beaches are magnificent.
Inland Trás-os-Montes, which means 'Beyond the Mountains',
(administrative districts of Bragança and Vila Real) consists
mainly of a high plateau cut by deep valleys. It is Portugal's
remotest area.

Douro, south of the Minho, comprises a small, mostly mountainous area round Oporto and is noted, like the Minho, for its
vinho verde (see p. 54) and its folklore. Inland, Beira
Alta (Guarda and Viseu) and Beira Baixa (Castelo Branco), east
and south-east of Douro, are the most mountain-filled areas of a
mountainous country: it is a sheep and cattle region, with
numerous towns and villages built in the shelter of ancient hilltop

castles, and with modern dams providing new sources of power and wealth. To all this Beira Litoral (Aveiro and Coimbra) provides a striking contrast. Much is low-lying and the shore consists of miles and miles of lovely white sand.

In the central area, Estremadura (Lisbon, Leiria, and Setúbal) was once Christian Portugal's 'extremity', as its name implies. Except for the Serra de Sintra and the Arrábida range, it is a region of rolling hills where you can see many of the country's most important ancient abbeys, palaces, and towns, including the capital. Its coast, broken by sporadic cliffs, includes Nazaré, Setúbal, and the long-established resorts of Estoril and Cascais. Inland from here the province of Ribatejo (Santarém) lies across the Tagus's lower valley. It is flattish alluvial land where fighting bulls are reared, and all manner of crops grown from vines to rice and vegetables.

The Alentejo is Portugal's largest province, covering a third of the country's total territory and divided into Alto or Upper (Portalegre and Evora) and Baixo or Lower (Beja). The Alentejo is often described as completely flat, which is quite untrue, as every car driver soon discovers. Castles and fortified towns perch on its higher hilltops; the big landowners' large, whitewashed farms, appropriately called *montes* ('hills'), occupy lower crests. Where the rolling open landscapes are not filled with grain crops they are thickly sprinkled with either cork or olive trees.

Separated from the Alentejo by a line of attractive low hills, the tiny, relatively flat Algarve is a world apart, a world of almonds and carobs, oranges, lemons, geraniums, aloes, agaves, sugar, cotton, and rice. Its tiny houses, though also painted white, are wholly different from the Alentejo's. The last bit of Portugal to be reconquered from the Moors, its towns and villages spread up the hillsides almost indistinguishably from the many 'white towns' of northern Morocco, founded, in some cases, by 13th-century Moorish refugees from the Algarve. Moorish influence is obvious too in the province's very distinctive and decorative chimney stacks and in relics such as the vast Moorish castle at Silves. And fringing its coast is another collection of lovely sandy beaches, the basis for large and rapidly growing tourist-residential developments like Vilamoura and Vale de Lobo, as well as some smaller centres.

Despite their differences, all provinces have two things in common —outstandingly friendly people and reasonable prices. And if you wonder why all these delights are only now becoming really popular the answer is simple—Portugal is only just beginning to have enough accommodation to cater for large-scale tourism. Even today it is hardly over-crowded with holiday-makers.

Lisbon

Lisbon is one of Europe's most beautiful cities. It lies on a number of south-facing low hills sloping down to the River Tagus at a point where the estuary is particularly wide and well-sheltered. The city's old medieval centre, Alfama, looks down on the modern centre to its west—the Baixa (Lower Town)—and across the Baixa to the Bairro Alto, with its lively shops and nightclubs. The main modern docks are at Alcántara, still further west, and beyond them at Belém superb 15th to 16th-century buildings mark the site of an older shipping centre. Today, though the city and its one million inhabitants have spread northward far from the river's bank, the Tagus has quaysides stretching all along the city's edge and it is still the artery that carries Lisbon's lifeblood.

Lisbon in fact owes its existence and its importance to its super-lative harbour. First occupied by Phoenicians some 3,000 years ago, it was in Roman hands for nearly six centuries and was a Moorish stronghold for four. It became part of Portugal in 1147, and in 1255 replaced Coimbra as the country's capital. In the 15th and early 16th centuries, at the time of the great discoveries, the city grew enormously in wealth and size, and was the starting-place for many notable voyages. Outstanding buildings at Belém recall those days of greatness. Lisbon once possessed many more buildings from the same period, but they were destroyed in the disastrous earthquake of 1755: on November 1st, while virtually the whole town was at High Mass, a violent earth tremor brought churches, houses, and other buildings crashing down. As fire spread through the ruins the survivors rushed to take refuge on the river. As they did so a huge tidal wave came upstream and engulfed the lower town. Some 40,000 of Lisbon's inhabitants were killed on that day.

Yet this same disaster allowed Lisbon to acquire much of its modern charm. For King José I's chief minister, later given the title of Marquis of Pombal, rebuilt the Baixa in a wholly revolutionary style. He conceived and laid out the straight streets inland from the Praça do Comercio and also built the elegant houses you still see today. He gave Lisbon, too, the magnificent Avenida da Liberdade, linking the squares inland from the Baixa to the Praça Marquês de Pombal named in his honour. Other areas, too, were laid out in similar manner, and Lisbon was endowed with an elegance that has been continued into modern times.

The city today has spread a long way north and east from the original central districts, and it is still growing. A whole range of new industries have been developed upstream towards Vila Franca de Xira, and the harbour and shipyards have spread to the Tagus's opposite bank.

The best place to start your sightseeing tour of Lisbon is undoubtedly the waterfront square officially called the Praça do Comercio, known to the Portuguese as Terreiro do Paço (Palace Terrace) from the former royal palace, and to the British and some other nationalities as Black Horse Square, because of the equestrian statue of King José I in its centre. As you stand here facing the Tagus, the bustling Sul e Sueste Station lies to your left front. The palace and the Baixa are behind you, the Cathedral, with Alfama beyond it, to your left, and the Bairro Alto behind and to your right. You can quickly get the feel of Lisbon by walking up one of the streets leading directly inland, such as the Rua Áurea or the Rua Augusta. Both lead into the busy square called the Rossio, with the Rossio Station, just beyond on the left. From the Rossio you pass straight on into the equally lively Praça dos Restauradores, with the Turismo office on your left, and the entrance to a very useful underground car park as well as to the most central of Lisbon's underground stations on the right. Without any break, Restauradores leads into the 1500-metre long and 90-metre wide Avenida da Liberdade (1 mile by almost 100 yards).

Avenida da Liberdade, Lisbon

A through road, flanked by gardens, runs down the middle, while the side roads are used by local traffic, including Lisbon's British-built double-decker buses. Shops, banks, offices, travel agents, and exchange offices fill all this area.

On your way up the Rua Aurea you will have passed a lift (Elevador) connecting with a high bridge leading to the Bairro Alto, and just beyond the Turismo office a funicular carries you up over the railway tunnel. The Bairro Alto itself is a sort of minor Baixa, noted chiefly for its nightspots and restaurants. The Rua Garrett, however, running downhill from the Largo do Chiado and usually called the Chiado, is Lisbon's Bond Street. Here you can see all the city's smartest shops and smartest people.

Medieval Lisbon can be enjoyed by going down the Rua da Madalena (parallel with the Rua Aurea on the Baixa's eastern edge) and bearing left up the hill at its end. This takes you past the Cathedral—built as a fortress at the end of the 12th century like those in Oporto, Coimbra, and Evora—and on along the Rua Barão to the Miradouro de Santa Luzia (St Lucia Belvedere). There is a good view from here of the little medieval streets, houses and churches of ancient Lisbon. From the belvedere you can go inland to St George's Castle (Castelo de São Jorge) or wander on through the narrow streets and stepped alleys of the colourful old houses of Alfama. This, the city's oldest part, still retains much of the layout it had during the Moorish occupation, before the numerous churches—still there—were built. Parts of the Moorish town wall can still be seen.

In the Largo das Portas do Sol (Sun Gate Square: the Sun Gate was one of the entrances to the Moorish city) the Fundação Ricardo Espirito Santa Silva, also called the Museum of Decorative Art, contains particularly interesting collections of 17th and 18th-century Portuguese and Indo-Portuguese furnishings, housed in a 17th-century palace.

Belém, west of the city centre, can be reached quickly by the road running beside the Tagus (take a taxi or a No. 15 tram from

Belém's decorative Manueline Tower

Black Horse Square if you do not have a car). The Belém Tower, the Jerónimos Monastery, the Museum of Ancient Art (Museu de Arte Antiga), the Museum of Popular Art (Museu de Arte Popular), and the modern monument to the Discoveries (Padrão dos Descobrimentos) make the expedition more than worthwhile. The Belém Tower is an almost unbelievably ornate building with a large gun-platform, erected in the middle of the harbour in 1515. Today it stands up against the shore because the contours have changed. To get the best view of it you need to see it from the water, and you can do this by taking one of the boat excursions that show you the whole of Lisbon's port.

The Jerónimos Monastery (Mosteiro dos Jerónimos: also called the Hieronymite Monastery) was started in 1502. It is one of the finest examples of Manueline design and contains also some Plateresque elements. Buildings added during the 19th century unfortunately seem rather out of place. While the church, dedicated to St Mary, is impressive, the magnificently ornate cloisters are completely overwhelming. The National Archaeological and Ethnographic Museum (Museu Nacional de Arqueologia e Etnografia) occupies one of the monastery's wings.

The National Museum of Ancient Art lies a little less than half-way between Black Horse Square and Belém, and can be visited on either the outward or the return journey. Its most famous painting is the polyptych of the Adoration of St Vincent by Nuno Gonçalves, painted in the mid-15th century. The museum contains gold and silver plate as well as paintings.

Of Lisbon's remaining famous sights, the 25 April Bridge and the view it provides as you approach the town, together with the enormous, soaring modern Christ in Majesty that you see to your left, cannot be omitted. And there are the beautiful Botanical Gardens on the Avenida da Liberdade, the park just beyond the Marquis of Pombal Square, the Cold Greenhouse (Estuga Fria)—a park with a magnificent view over the town and the river; in addition to many other museums, churches and gardens.

But even if you look at none of Lisbon's special sights you will still find it an extraordinarily pleasant place to be in. Merely walking through the streets—whether old or new—sitting in the gardens, taking boat trips on the river, enjoying the restaurants and nightspots—including the 'fado restaurants' (see p. 30)—is occupation enough.

Albufeira

Albufeira today is a popular small coastal holiday town in the central Algarve. Its picturesque, white-painted centre, perched on the headland (pierced by a tunnel) which separates the Bathers' and Fishermen's Beaches, has been occupied for over 2000 years by Greeks, Romans, Moors, and Portuguese in succession. Apart from nightclubs, restaurants, bars, boutiques, and hotels (some on beaches to the east of the town), local colour and bargains are provided by the daily fruit and vegetable market, at its best early on Sunday, and the daily fish market, where catches brought in by the gaily-painted boats are sold. Albufeira is also the centre for the Clube Praia da Oura and other smaller residential and holiday developments. Good riding can be enjoyed at some of these.

Alcobaça

A quiet commercial country town, set among vast fruit orchards about 97 km north of Lisbon in a region which also produces attractive pottery, Alcobaça is world-famous for its magnificent Santa Maria Monastery. Building, by Cistercian monks, began in 1178 in fulfilment of a vow made by King Alfonso I after his capture of Santarém from the Moors in 1147.

The church has been restored to reveal its original clean lines and spaciousness. The adjacent Cloister of Silence (14th century with 16th-century upper storey) is also impressive in its simplicity. Beyond the cloister one can visit the monks' quarters.

The church's transepts contain the magnificently carved tombs of King Pedro I and his Castilian wife Inês de Castro, whom he had married secretly in 1345, while still Crown Prince, on the death of his first wife, Princess Constanza of Castile. King Afonso IV, Pedro's father, fearing Castilian influence and not knowing of the marriage, banished her from the Portuguese court. When Pedro continued to visit her in Coimbra she was murdered. Pedro rebelled against his father and two years later became king. He had the hearts of his wife's murderers torn from their living bodies and brought to him. Six years after Inês's death, her body, then buried in Coimbra, was exhumed and crowned and the court forced to pay homage to the decomposing corpse.

Alcobaça can be visited during a long day's excursion from Lisbon, Estoril, or Cascais.

Algarve resorts

A lot of trouble occurs, especially among readers of tour operators' brochures, because many resorts listed in them are either former hamlets technically part of larger conurbations or are main towns that have been swamped in holiday makers' minds by newer hamlet-based resorts. To save space and, we hope, confusion, we deal with Almancil (Almansil), Quinta do Lago, and Vilamoura under **Quarteira.** Alvor, Montes de Alvor, Penina, Burgau, Salema and

Praia dos Tres Irmãos are treated as part of **Portimão.** Cape St
Vincent is dealt with under Sagres, and Praia da Oura under
Albufeira.

Almourol Castle

A romantic-looking fortress on a tiny island in the River Tagus,
about 120 km from Lisbon. Well worth a visit.

Amarante

Amarante is a pleasant small northern town set among the
mountains and vineyards of the Douro region. The wooden
balconies and iron window-grilles of the 17th to 18th-century
houses give the town a very attractive appearance.

Armacao de Pera

This striking, completely modern Algarve resort, reached by a side
road from the old village of Pera just west of Albufeira, has one of
the Algarve's pleasantest and safest sandy beaches, set in a small
bay ringed by low hills.

Arrábida, Serra da

West of Setúbal, barely 40 km south of Lisbon, the Serra da
Arrábida rises suddenly along the coast towards Cape Espichel out
of an almost completely flat plain. Reaching heights of 500 m
(1600 feet) in places, it slopes steeply to the sea but less sharply
to the north. Towards the sea the slopes are covered with arbutus,
myrtle, and other Mediterranean shrubs, with pines, cypresses, and
a mass of different trees above them. Vineyards, olive groves, and
fruit trees cover the northern slopes.

Aveiro

The old town of Aveiro, busy now, lies in a landscape you do not
expect to find in Portugal—a completely flat expanse of salt
marshes, saltwater lagoons, sandbars, and canals. Outside the
town, centuries-old saltpans still produce high-quality sea-salt, rice
is extensively grown, and cattle are grazed on rich marshlands.
It possesses also large-scale canneries. For visitors, however, the
waterways surrounding the town and the vast sandy beaches 8 km
to the west are the chief attraction. The former Convent of Jesus
has been made into an interesting regional museum. Aveiro is at its
best during the March feira, when *moliceiros* (local boats) sail down
the City Canal.

Barcelos

The colourful little inland town of Barcelos, close to the coast
between Viana do Castelo and Oporto, is famous for its cock, sold
as a good luck emblem throughout Portugal. The story goes that a
pilgrim making his way towards Santiago de Compostela was
convicted of theft in Barcelos. Condemned to die but knowing

himself innocent he declared that the cock which the judge was about to eat would stand up and crow to prove him right. It did, and in gratitude the pilgrim presented the town with a carved and decorated cock which can be seen in Barcelos' archaeological museum.

Batalha

About 120 km north of Lisbon, on the N1, you can see, rising from a small valley, the forest of pinnacles, buttresses, and turrets of the magnificent monastery of Batalha. It was built by João I in fulfilment of a vow he made before the battle of Aljubarrota, fought against the Castilian claimant to the Portuguese throne in 1385. The monastery took over 150 years to build so that it is a mixture of different styles, all of which, however, blend extremely harmoniously.

The church is a magnificent soaring Gothic structure, with the later Founders' Chapel, to the right of the main entrance, designed in Flamboyant. The Royal Cloister north of the church is a very striking mixture of Gothic and ornate Manueline. Leading off the cloister, the Chapter House with its superb vaulting—almost 20 m (66 feet) without intermediate supports—contains the shrine of the Portuguese Unknown Soldier.

The Founders' Chapel is interesting to both Portuguese and British visitors: in it lies the beautiful joint tomb of João I and his queen, Philippa, daughter of John of Gaunt. She and her husband founded the royal line that ruled Portugal till modern times. Their children, including Prince Henry the Navigator, are also buried here. The precinct around Batalha Monastery has numerous shops selling the pottery for which Estremadura province is famous. But the lack of shade can be trying.

Beja

Beja is a busy country town of white houses and new flats standing on a hill that rises a little above the Alentejo plateau. It is the capital of Lower Alentejo. Originally a Roman city, it was occupied for four centuries by Moors before becoming a fortress town designed to repel attacks from Spain. You can still visit the 13th-century castle. The 15th-century former Convent of the Conception today houses the regional museum.

Berlenga Island

Tiny Berlenga Island lies 12 km off the coast north of Lisbon and is reached in about an hour by regular boat services from Peniche. Its granite coastline is surrounded by caves, reefs, and even smaller islands. Boats can be hired to make trips round the island. Berlenga is specially famous for its underwater fishing, and possesses a simple pousada.

Braga

Important since Roman times, Braga is a main centre of the modern Minho province. It is an inland town, built on hills and famous on three counts: for fine ecclesiastical architecture; for its celebration of the Feast of St John the Baptist on June 23rd and 24th each year; and for its weekly Tuesday market, at which local craftsmen's products can be bought.

The Cathedral contains architecture of every period from the 12th to 18th centuries. The Treasury is divided into two parts, one containing mainly 18th-century church vestments, and the other a notable collection of 16th-century azulejos. Amongst the chapels, one contains fine 17th-century azulejos, and another 14th-century wall paintings in Mudéjar style. Small admission charges are made for each part of the Treasury, and collectively for the chapels.

The former Episcopal Palace (Antigo Paço Episcopal), another notable building, dates from the 14th, 16th, and 18th centuries, and contains one of Portugal's richest libraries, with documents going back to the 9th century. There are several other churches and buildings in Braga of architectural interest, many with azulejos.

Bragança

Old Bragança, the walled administrative centre of the remote north-eastern province of Trás-os-Montes, boasts Portugal's oldest town hall (12th-century), built to a pentagonal ground-plan; a 12th-century castle which dominates the old town and provides superb views from its keep; and a highly decorated pillory. It is 680 m above sea level, and the modern town is located on lower ground.

Bussaco

Bussaco (Buçaco in Portuguese) is famous for its mountain forest and for Wellington's victory over Napoleonic troops in 1810. The forest has been notable since the 6th century, when Benedictine monks established a hermitage among the original oaks and pines. They tended the trees carefully, and when the Carmelites built a monastery on the site of the present hotel in 1628 they planted new varieties that included maple, cedars, laurels, amongst others. In 1834, when the religious orders were banned in Portugal, the government took over the forest and introduced even more varied planting. Today at Bussaco you can see 400 varieties of native trees and about 300 exotic species. Eucalyptus, pine, oak, monkey-puzzle trees, cedars, thuyas, oriental spruces, sequoias, Japanese camphor trees, and a great deal more flourish here. Bussaco lies about 30 km north of Coimbra by road, and possesses a hotel.

Caldas da Rainha

This quiet little spa town—'the Queen's Spa'—took its name from João II's queen in 1484. Seeing country people bathing in foul-smelling pools at the roadside, she stopped, tried them for herself, and was so pleased with the results that she stayed on. Later she founded a hospital and a church in the town and ordered a large park to be laid out. The Spa Park, still delightful, has a good campsite.

Caldas is a pleasant touring base for the region north of Lisbon.

Cape St Vincent See Sagres.

Carcavelos See Estoril.

Cascais

The ancient fishing port of Cascais, at the foot of the Sintra hills just west of Lisbon, began its transformation into the popular resort it is today in the summer of 1870, when the court moved there for the first time. It stands on a wide bay with a beautiful sandy beach. Inland, mountains slope sharply up from the town, providing cooling breezes in summer. A former royal palace, then one of the President's residences, stands on the promontory to the south-west. A good entertainment and excursion centre.

The stretch of coast running west from Lisbon, on which Cascais, Estoril and other resorts stands, is called the Costa do Sol.

Castelo de Vide

A former fortress town among the hills close to the Spanish frontier on the main road (N118) from Santarém, Castelo de Vide has retained its 12th-century castle and ancient Jewish quarter.

Chaves

This charming hillside town, once a frontier fortress, climbs from the Roman bridge over the Tâmega up to the town square. It provides a delightful welcome to Portugal, 10 km from the Spanish frontier by the N2.

Coimbra

The medieval city centre of Coimbra, Portugal's third largest city, rises in tiers on a steep hill beside the River Mondego. Coimbra was Portugal's first capital and from 1308 has been the home of one of Europe's oldest universities. The old town is picturesque, with narrow winding streets and numerous fine buildings, and occupies a special place in the history and affections of the Portuguese people. During the university terms the presence of several thousand students, wearing black gowns and coloured faculty ribbons—the university teachers also wear special caps—gives the town an even more romantic appearance. Coimbra has plenty of hotels and restaurants and is a good centre for visiting the three Beira provinces.

Most places of interest are concentrated in the old town and in the newer suburb on the other side of the River Mondego, close to the wide Ponte Santa Clara. To visit the old town first, start in the large triangular 'square' opposite the bridge's end, and walk away from the river till you see on your right the 12th-century Almedina Gate. Turn through it and then keep round left past the Sub Ripas and Arco mansions, both private residences. The first was built in Manueline style early in the 16th century; the second has a fine Renaissance courtyard. Turn right a little past the two houses and then right again up the Rua dos Coutinhos till you come to the Old Cathedral (Sé), a fortress-like building, except for its decorated north door, added later and subsequently badly damaged. The Cathedral was, in fact, erected as a fortress in the mid-12th century when Portugal was still busily fighting the Moors, but it now shows traces of every style of architecture from Romanesque onwards, including Gothic, Baroque, and Mudéjar.

Beyond the Cathedral the former Bishop's Palace now houses the Machado de Castro art museum.

Past the museum, the Rua Sá de Miranda brings you into the main university area. The Old University lies further along to your right. The Old University's library (ring for admission), built in 1724 is a fine piece of Baroque architecture, with ceilings painted in false perspective. Its Manueline chapel is specially famous for the highly decorated door and its fine 17th-century azulejos.

The Monastery of the Holy Cross (Mosteiro de Santa Cruz) lies about 200 m north of the Almedina Gate (continue along the Rua Ferreira Borges leading from the Ponte Santa Clara), and dates from the 16th century. The interior contains much fine architecture. The cloister is a beautiful example of Manueline design.

On the Mondego's other bank you can visit the Old Convent of St Clare (Santa Clara a Velha), where Inês de Castro's body (see Alcobaça) was buried till its transfer to Alcobaça; and also the New Convent of St Clare (Santa Clara a Nova) with its fine Baroque church which contains the 14th-century tomb of Queen St Isabel. The Park of Tears (Quinta das Lagrimas), a small and rather lovely wooded area where Inês de Castro is said to have been murdered, lies about 500 m down the road towards Lisbon. Between them, in very different vein, stands Children's Portugal (Portugal dos Pequenitos), a delightful park containing models of many of Portugal's main historic monuments as well as models of typical houses from both Portugal and its overseas territories.

Popular short excursions from Coimbra take visitors to Bussaco Forest (above), and the Roman remains at Conimbriga (see below).

Conimbriga

The remains of Roman Conimbriga, 15 km south-west of Coimbra, are impressive and give a comprehensive idea of the town as it was in about the 4th century AD. The site was occupied by Celts during the Iron Age. The Roman town was captured by barbarian invaders in AD 468, and lost its importance after the foundation of modern Coimbra.

Douro Valley

Both the Douro Valley itself and the long vine-covered mountain slopes stretching for many miles on either side of the river are notably colourful and picturesque. The area through which the lower river runs down to the sea at Oporto, from just above Resende, is noted for the light sparkling white *vinho verde* (green wine) made from grapes that never mature fully. Port wine comes from grapes grown in the upper valley, stretching as far as the Spanish frontier (see Oporto).

While the whole region is exceptionally beautiful and most side roads well worth exploring, one drive is particularly popular, and takes visitors along the left (southern) bank from Souselo to Pinhão, by the N222, and then northward to Vila Real, with a call en route at the Mateus estate near Vila Real, famous throughout Europe for its rosé wine.

Elvas

Only a few miles from the Spanish frontier and the Spanish fortress town of Badajoz, Elvas is famous throughout Portugal chiefly for its superb sugar plums. It deserves, however, to be far more widely known, both for its magnificent fortifications—an excellent and impressive example of 17th-century military architecture—and for the beauty of its old white houses, narrow streets, and charming squares. If you have a car it is well worth driving round the ramparts. On the way you will see an aqueduct, begun in the 15th century, which still carries water to the town.

Go into the town from the south and make for the archway (Arco do Relogio). Go through this into the Praça de Sancho II. The former Town Hall stands on one side and the former Cathedral on the other. A street on the right of the Cathedral leads to another delightful square, the Largo Santa Clara, where you can see a fine example of one of Portugal's many 16th-century pillories, a 16th-century Renaissance church containing some specially attractive 17th-century azulejos, and also remains of the original 10th-century Moorish fortifications. If you continue uphill you come to the Castle. Built originally by the Moors, it was altered and strengthened in the 14th-16th centuries. A wonderful view of the town and the surrounding countryside can be had from the ramparts. There is a state pousada in the town.

Espinho See Porto.

Estoril

Estoril on the Costa do Sol, reached in under half-an-hour from Lisbon by fast electric train, is Portugal's largest and most fashionable coast resort. The town, looking across the bay to Cascais, 3 km away, is elegantly and attractively built, and its park contains a wealth of exotic tropical plants. Estoril provides almost everything that holidaymakers could wish for—including good hotels and restaurants, and plentiful excursions to places like Lisbon, Sintra, Cascais, Obidos, Batalha, and Carcavelos, a more modest resort, 7 km from Estoril towards Lisbon. The climate is mild in winter, and in summer the heat is tempered by breezes from the mountains.

The fashionable Estoril seafront

Estrela, Serra da

Of all of Portugal's innumerable mountain chains, the Serra da Estrela is the most grandiose and impressive. 60 km long and 30 wide, rising to a height of nearly 2000 m (over 6,500 feet), it consists mostly of vast treeless plateaux, boulder-strewn cliff-like slopes, and frighteningly deep gorges. The rebuilt road between Seia and Covilhã is particularly impressive. It passes close by Torre, the range's highest peak. A modern ski resort is taking shape at Penhas da Saude, which you pass on this route. Simple accommodation is available at both Seia and Covilhã.

Estremoz

Estremoz, another of the Upper Alentejo's beautiful fortified towns, lies about 50 km further from Elvas on the main road running from Badajoz in Spain through Elvas to Lisbon. Dominated by its medieval castle and 17th-century ramparts, Estremoz is today famous for the pottery manufactured there, and also for its figurines. Scores of stalls sell them at the market held on Saturdays.

A good regional museum stands in the main square known as the Rossio, with two pillories close by. From here you can walk into the old town and up to the Castle and King Dinis I's palace, now a pousada. The castle chapel contains lovely azulejos that tell the story of Queen St Isabel of Aragon, King Dinis's wife. St Mary's Church, which is square, formed part of the original citadel.

Evora

Evora, some 48 km south-west of Estremoz, is the largest and most famous of all the Alentejo's famous fortified towns. The city walls are vast and impressive. Many of the old town's cobbled streets are as narrow and winding as those you find in any Moorish medina, though the houses are often beautifully built and adorned with their former owners' coats-of-arms. The Cathedral (Sé) stands at the top of the hill in the town centre, with the remains of a Roman temple, dedicated to Diana the goddess of hunting, at a slightly higher level. There was once a university in the town.

Roman temple and Cathedral at Evora

A street running south from the cathedral takes you to the famous Moura Gates Square (Largo das Portas de Moura), where you can see a delightful Renaissance fountain, some aristocratic houses, and part of the town's medieval fortifications.

The Rua da Republica, leading to the railway station, contains two of the town's more interesting churches: the São Francisco, built in a local version of Gothic-Manueline style and including an extraordinary ossuary chapel with hundreds of monks' skeletons set into the wall; and the São Bras Hermitage, a Gothic-Mudejar building dating from 1480.

These are only the outstanding items, suitable for a quick visit. Evora deserves a longer stay and more detailed exploration. The Turismo office provides excellent town plans free. It is also a good centre from which to explore the unusual Upper Alentejo region with its many fortified towns, such as Elvas, Estremoz, and Evoramonte, to name a few.

Evoramonte

This small, and extraordinarily attractive fort town occupies a hilltop in the mountain region between Evora and Estremoz. It is dominated by its castle—containing Roman, Moorish, and mediaeval portions—on the top of its hill.

Faro

A busy commercial and fishing centre in the centre of the Algarve coast, Faro is the province's modern capital, as well as an important tourist centre. Though separated from the open sea by a large lagoon bounded by sandbars, Faro's port is still lively and busy. The international airport serving the whole Algarve lies 4 km west of the town.

Faro was an important city when it was captured from the Moors in 1249. Two hundred years later its Jewish community printed Portugal's first books. The town was sacked by British naval forces in 1596, during the period when Portugal formed part of Spain. It was damaged by an earthquake in 1722, and the great 'quake of 1755 reduced it to ruins once again. Bishop Dom Francisco Gomes, commemorated by an obelisk in the square close to the harbour named after him, fought hard for its reconstruction and is largely responsible for the town's present prosperity.

The tiny original town lies south of the harbour. Though the ramparts have disappeared their position can be clearly seen in the ring of houses surrounding the area. The Cathedral, containing notable azulejos, occupies the old town's central point, with a square lined with orange trees to one side. An entertaining Maritime Museum (Museu Maritimo) lies off one side of the square. Models of various types of fishing boats form its chief attraction.

In the busy new town to the north the Rua de Santo António contains a number of fashionable boutiques and shops. The small Ethnological Museum has exhibits that deal very effectively with all the Algarve's traditional handicrafts and everyday life.

At the town's main beach, Praia de Faro, you can surf on the sandbar's open side, and water-ski in the lagoon's calmer waters.

Faro is a good yachting centre. Boats, however, cannot be hired, though excursions can be arranged with local fishermen.

Fátima

Twenty km from Batalha and about 150 from Lisbon, this little town's world-wide fame is derived from remarkable events that occurred in May 1917. Three local children, watching their parents' sheep grazing a mile from the village, had a vision of a beautiful lady who promised she would come back on the 13th of each month until October, when she would reveal who she was. When news of the children's story reached the Lisbon papers, every sort of pressure was put on them by the anti-clerical authorities of the time, but they stuck unshakeably to their original account. Their firmness created such an impression that on October 12th a crowd of over 70,000 people gathered at Fátima, hoping to see the vision for themselves.

On the morning of the 13th the weather was terrible. The sky was covered with thick cloud, and it rained heavily. No one except the eldest of the children, Lucia, saw the vision, but everyone saw the sun suddenly appear through the clouds and seem to revolve like a ball of fire. Lucia said that the vision had revealed itself as Our Lady of the Rosary and had ordered a chapel to be built on the spot, where the people of the world could come to do penance for their terrible sin—taken as a reference to World War I. The two younger children died in the influenza epidemic of 1919-20 and are buried in the basilica built in accordance with the vision's command. Lucia became a nun and still lives in a convent near Coimbra. The events were formally recognised as miraculous by the Roman Catholic church authorities in 1930, and Fátima became an official place of pilgrimage.

On the 12th of every month from May to October, huge numbers of pilgrims assemble and go in procession along the wide esplanade leading to the basilica with its 65 m-high tower. Masses are celebrated inside and outside the basilica, at which tens of thousands of people receive Communion together. Many who are sick also come to be healed. Apart from the basilica and the esplanade leading to it, a shrine near the evergreen oak in which the vision appeared—the present tree is a replacement—contains a statue of the Virgin. The spot where a spring came suddenly from the ground, on the occasion of the vision's final appearance, is marked by a column.

As a town, Fátima has no great distinction. There are, of course, plenty of places where visitors can be accommodated.

Figueira da Foz

A huge beach of fine white sand lines Figueira Bay at the mouth of the River Mondego, about 45 km west of Coimbra. The new part of the town, to the west, is one of the seaside resorts most popular with Portuguese holidaymakers and offers a wide choice of leisure occupations, sport, and entertainment. The town's celebration of the Feast of St John the Baptist on June 23rd-24th is a very colourful occasion.

Figueira's eastern half is still devoted largely to the centuries-old sardine and cod-fishing industries, and to shipyards. A range of hills to the north, the Serra da Bôa Viagem, provides a wonderful view of the town and of the saltmarshes to the south from its highest point. A circular drive, going westward towards Cape Mondego (Cabo Mondego), and then inland towards the viewpoint, takes you past the picturesque little fishing village of Buarcos.

Figueira is a good centre from which to visit Coimbra, Fátima, Aveiro, Batalha, Alcobaça, etc. Historians know it as the place where Wellington landed his first troops in August 1808, after the fort which still overlooks Figueira Bay had been captured by Coimbra students.

Guarda

Guarda, 54 km from Spain on the main road leading eastward from Viseu and Coimbra, is Portugal's highest town—1040 m (over 3,400 feet) above sea level on one of the Serra da Estrela's foothills. Once it was the main fortress of the province of Beira Alta. Today it is an administrative centre and mountain resort. The 14th to 18th-century Cathedral has some attractive corners. Aristocratic houses ornamented with former owners' coats-of-arms can be seen in the Cathedral square and in Rua do Dom Luis I leading off it.

Guimarães

Guimarães is an inland town not far from the coast in the Minho province. Founded in the 10th century, it consisted originally of little more than a monastery with a defensive tower. Today it is a flourishing commercial centre whose industries include textiles, tanning, jewellery-making, pottery, embroidery, the manufacture of cutlery and kitchenware, and the carving of the highly decorative wooden yokes that you see on the necks of all the oxen pulling carts in the Minho region. Portugal's first king was born at Guimarães in about 1112. The writer Gil Vicente was born in the town in 1470.

The enormously tall 10th-century tower still dominates the town that has grown around it. It stands at the top of a hill whose slopes have been turned into a pleasant public park with the Dukes' Palace (Paço dos Duques) to the south, and the old town's centre beyond it. The long Largo da Republica do Brasil contains a fine mosaic pavement, such as is found in many Portuguese towns, and is surrounded by picturesque old houses.

The Castle was thoroughly restored in 1940. The views from it are magnificent. A small Romanesque chapel, where Portugal's first king was baptised, stands near the Castle. The Palace of the Dukes of Bragança, usually known as the Paço dos Duques, is only a little further away. It is a lavishly decorated 15th-century house, open to the public, and containing notable tapestries, paintings, and furniture. There are many other notable old buildings.

Lagoa

Lagoa, an attractive inland Algarve town between Portimão and Albufeira, is known chiefly as a wine-producing centre, though it also offers a strategically-situated motel.

Lagos

Lagos, near the western end of the Algarve coast, lies on a wide estuary, well sheltered from Atlantic gales by the Ponta da Piedade promontory. It is an extremely colourful small town, whose strong fortifications still surround the central area. A tiny 15th-century fort that once protected the harbour, still filled with colourful fishing vessels, is linked to the land by a drawbridge.

Lagos, today, is an important fishing centre, with a sizeable canning industry, and is also the centre of a rice-growing region. Historically, it is famous chiefly as the starting point of Prince Henry the Navigator's 15th-century voyages (see p. 31). A statue of Gil Eanes, or Eannes, overlooks the harbour in front of the town's main entrance. He was the first man to sail further south than Cape Bojador, on Africa's west coast, then the known world's limit.

St Anthony's Church (Igreja Santo António), a little beyond the larger church overlooking the harbour, despite its plain facade is filled with extraordinarily exuberant Baroque decoration—the ceiling pointed in false relief and the walls covered with gilded wood-carving.

Modern resort developments for which Lagos serves as a main centre include Luz Bay on the Praia da Luz, about 6 km west; the

Ponta da Piedade, 2 km due south; the Praia de Dona Ana and
Meia Praia to the east; together with new accommodation in the
tiny fishing villages of Burgau and Salema, 4 and 8 km respectively
beyond Luz Bay. But these occupy only six of the many sandy
beaches stretching along the coast on either side of Lagos.

Lamego
Small town in pleasant countryside 40 km south of Vila Real,
famous for its baroque sanctuary reached by a long, magnificently
balustraded stone staircase.

Leiria
Roughly 130 km north of Lisbon on the main Oporto road (N1),
Leiria is a pretty country town on the River Liz. Its two halves
are connected by a Roman bridge, still in use. Both the town and
the surrounding region are dominated by a great castle, open to
the public, started in 1135 by Afonso I, Portugal's first king, on a
plateau high above the town. The view from its battlements
extends seawards over the great forest planted by King Dinis I
in the 13th century to prevent winter gales spreading sand inland.
Leira today is famous for its handicrafts and its folklore. Many
women still wear their traditional costume. The region's folk-
dancing can be seen at its best during Leiria's annual fair (end of
March-early April).

Loulé
Loulé is a busy inland commercial and manufacturing town in the
central Algarve, typical in style, and noted for its Carnival and
Almond Gatherers' Fair that starts each year on the Saturday
before Shrove Tuesday and lasts 4 days.

Mafra
The plateau town of Mafra, 45 km north of Lisbon, and half-
way between Sintra and Torres Vedras (see below), has grown up
beside an enormous monastery whose construction was ordered
in 1717 by King João V. The building was in thanksgiving for the
birth of a daughter, and is on an extraordinarily lavish scale. It
covers 4 hectares (10 acres). Building materials for it came from
Portugal, Belgium, France, Italy, Holland, and Brazil. 50,000 men
worked on it, and construction lasted 13 years. Its frontage of
220 m (over 260 yards) is greater even than that of the famous
El Escorial monastery near Madrid, built 1563-84, which, it is said,
Mafra was intended to rival. With so many foreign architects and
artists gathered in Mafra for the monastery's construction, King
João took the opportunity to found there a school of sculpture,
whose teachers, then and later, included many famous artists
whose works can be seen throughout Portugal.

You can visit the superb marble basilica that forms the central point

in the frontage, and also parts of the former palace and monastery.
Notable features in the basilica include the jasper and marble
altarpieces and the superb, lofty pink and white marble cupola.
In the palace and monastery you can see the monks' cells, their
kitchens, hospital, and pharmacy, the royal apartments, one of the
sculpture studios, and the magnificent library housed in a vast
Baroque gallery containing some 35,000 volumes.

Marvão
A striking medieval former fortress town among the hills near the
Spanish border, on the Santarém road (N118), 22 km from
Portalegre and 8 km from Castelo de Vide.

Miranda do Douro
Miranda do Douro is perched picturesquely above a sheer drop
to the River Douro and the Spanish frontier in Portugal's remotest
north-eastern corner. It is famous for its traditional Pauliteiros
sword dance, best seen at the annual *romaria* to the shrine of Our
Lady of Nazo (*Nossa Senhora de Nazo*) at the village of Povoa,
11 km north of Miranda, on September 7th and 8th.

Monchique
The hills which separate the Algarve and Alentejo provinces reach
their highest point— 902 m, almost 3000 feet— at Mount Fóia in
the Serra de Monchique in the western Algarve. The road running
north from Portimão or Silves through carobs, arbutus, and wild
rhododendrons, as well as fields of cotton and sugar, is particularly
attractive; while the view from the heights extends to Portimão,
Lagos, and Cape St Vincent.

Monte Gordo
Once a prosperous small fishing village on the Algarve coast's
eastern end, beside the mouth of the River Guadiana, Monte
Gordo has developed into a large and important modern coast
resort, thanks mainly to its enormous beach of fine white sand and
the pines that cover large areas of the surrounding countryside.

Nazaré
Nazaré, one of Portugal's and Europe's most famous and most
photographed fishing ports, lies about 120 km north of Lisbon in a
cliff-bound bay on the Estremadura coast. It owes its fame partly
to its position but mainly to the colourful activities of the fishermen.
Both men and women wear mainly black woollen garments.
Their boats are painted with brilliant colours in designs that
sometimes recall the themes of ancient magic. With their high
prows and sterns, designed to protect them against being over-
whelmed by the steep Atlantic rollers, they look as though they

may well have been derived from the Phoenicians—the first, as far as we know, to settle in Nazaré. The beach has no protecting breakwater or sheltered harbour and launching the boats into the Atlantic surf, for all the regularity with which it is accomplished, invariably strikes visitors as a near-miraculous feat. Hauling the boats back on shore when they return with their catches—oxen are still used—is no less spectacular. Everyone within reach, including tourists (if they want the locals' goodwill) helps. A siren sounds the starting signal. And once the catch is safely ashore the women carry vast loads of fish on their heads to the fish market— though much of the catch nowadays goes to the town's flourishing canneries.

The upper town, the Sítio (O Sítio), most easily reached from the beach by a funicular, is perched on the top of one of Portugal's highest cliffs, some 110 m (over 350 feet) above the sea. The northern part of the lower town, known as A Praia (The Beach), contains the narrow streets and tiny houses of the fishermen's quarter, while the new town, called Pederneira, stretches southwards beside the gigantic sandy beach. The best view of the town and its beach is the one from the belvedere built into the Sítio's cliffside.

With its fine beach (though poor bathing), Nazaré has naturally become a holiday resort popular with Portuguese and discerning foreign visitors. Riding, tennis, and boat excursions are available.

Obidos

Obidos is an enchanting, tiny, medieval walled town filled with white-painted houses. It is situated on an inland hilltop about 45 km south of Nazaré. The walls date from the time of the

Obidos: Church of Santa Maria in the main square

Moorish occupation, but were extended by the Portuguese in the 12th, 13th, and 16th centuries, following the capture of the town in 1148. In recent years a lot of restoration work has been done, and the tiny town now earns its living purely from tourism. But that does not prevent it being one of Europe's most charming and worthwhile tourist traps. The winding streets, the ring of ancient ramparts, and the town's churches that date from the 15th century on, are well set off by flowers that grow everywhere in great profusion.

King Dinis I visited Obidos in 1228, accompanied by his wife, Queen St Isabel. She was so enchanted by the little town that the King gave it to her as a present. Subsequent Portuguese kings continued the tradition of presenting Obidos to their Queens until as late as 1833. In the 16th century the castle at the highest point of the town became a royal residence. More recently it was transformed into a delightful pousada that makes a wonderful touring base—provided you do not mind its rather steep medieval stairs.

Obidos is excellently placed for car trips to all the main places of interest in Estremadura province, and features in many coach excursions from Lisbon, Estoril, Cascais, etc.

Olhão

A busy little sardine-fishing and canning port on the Algarve coast some 8 km east of Faro, Olhão is known to visitors mainly as a picturesque town of innumerable white and blue cube-shaped houses. Unfortunately they are being increasingly hidden from sight by taller—and duller—modern buildings. Olhão is a minor resort as well as a fishing port. Like Faro it lies on a lagoon. Its beach, on the sandbar enclosing the lagoon, is reached by ferry.

Oporto

The town's name, usually written plain Porto ('Port') in modern Portuguese (O Porto means 'The Port'), derives from the twin Roman towns of Portus and Cale which once stood on opposite shores of the River Douro. Portus-Cale or Portucale, as the base from which the Moorish invaders were driven out, also gave its name to the modern country.

Later in history, Oporto fitted out the expedition of Prince Henry the Navigator which captured the town of Ceuta on the Moroccan Mediterranean coast, in 1415—the start of Portugal's great era of discovery and conquest. The requisitioning of all the local cattle to feed the troops had a curious result—if a long-standing tradition can be believed. The fighting men took all the meat, and the local people, left with the offal, developed a taste for tripe. *Tripas à modo do Porto*—tripe cooked the Oporto way—is still a popular dish and the people of the town are still referred to by other Portuguese as *tripeiros* (tripe-eaters).

Oporto today, with some 350,000 inhabitants, ranks as Portugal's second city. It occupies a lovely site on hills sloping down to the Douro's northern bank a few km before the river joins the sea. In former times the wide Douro formed something of a barrier to communications with the country to its north. Today Oporto is linked to the opposite shore by three notable bridges. The oldest and furthest upstream, the Dona Maria Pia railway bridge, was built entirely of cast iron in 1877 by the French engineer Eiffel, of Eiffel Tower fame. The second, the Dom Luis I road bridge, ingeniously serves both upper and lower town levels on both banks of the river by carrying two roads over the water. The third, the Arrábida road bridge furthest downstream, carries the modern motorway across the river in a single concrete span of almost 270 m (295 yards)—a world record at the time of its construction in 1953.

Both road bridges provide interesting views as you approach the town. The Dom Luis I bridge leads directly into the old town centre, with most of the places of interest to the left as you arrive. In an area little more than 800 m (about half-a-mile) square you can see the old city's picturesque alleys leading up to the Cathedral Square, the Cathedral itself with the former Bishop's Palace beside it, Prince Henry the Navigator's House, the Stock Exchange (containing a mock-Moorish hall), the Ethnographic Museum, the São Francisco Church with its overpoweringly magnificent Baroque interior, the so-called 'English Factory'—now serving as a club for British wine-merchants, and the Clérigos church's lofty tower.

The Cathedral began its existence as a 12th-century fortress church. Its severe exterior gives little hint of the 16th to 17th-century splendour inside. The 14th-century cloisters adjoining it to the south, are decorated with 18th-century azulejos illustrating the life of the Virgin and scenes from the Roman poet Ovid's *Metamorphoses*—a juxtaposition which probably seemed quite normal at the time.

The main road that the Dom Luis I bridge runs into leads north into the enormous double avenue composed of the Praça da Liberdade, the Avenida dos Aliados, and the Praça do Municipio, with a very grand Town Hall at its end (the Turismo office at pavement level on the right-hand corner provides free maps and information). The city's main shopping and commercial area is spread around this central space.

Avenida dos Aliados, Oporto

To the British, Oporto is more or less synonymous with port wine. However, the wineries are all on the Douro's other bank, in the suburb of Vila Nova de Gaia. They all keep open house to visitors except on Sundays and public holidays and, in some cases, Saturday afternoons. Here you will be taken round and shown the immense vats in which the maturing process begins. Initial fermentation and the addition of the brandy which puts a halt to it, retaining some of the grape's natural sugar, takes place before the wine comes down the Douro in barges to Vila Nova. For over 200 years the British have been the main customers for dessert, or tawny, port—the Portuguese and others drink also the dry white port as an aperitif—and many of the great shipping firms have been controlled by the same Anglo-Portuguese families for a century or more. Free tastings are included.

There is far more to see in Oporto than we have space to describe in detail here. Other museums and ancient churches, for instance, fine parks, the vast new harbour at Leixões nearer the sea, and the lively resort-suburbs of Foz do Douro, south of Leixões, and Matosinhos to its north. Espinho, 16 km south, has a good beach and a golf course.

Peniche

About 25 km west of Obidos, Peniche is Portugal's third most important fishing port, where crayfish, tunny, sardines, and other catches are landed and canned. The town has long been famous for pillow-lace. Peniche is also the embarkation point for the 1-hour journey to Berlenga Island (see above). The Citadel, built to command the approach to the 2-km long Cape Carvoeiro promontory, has retained its 17th-century ramparts almost intact.

Penina See Portimão.

Pombal

Pombal is a small town about 45 km south of Coimbra on the main road between Lisbon and Oporto. It possesses a castle originally built in the 12th century by a Grand Master of the Knights Templar

Portalegre

Only a few km from Marvão, Castelo de Vide, and the Spanish frontier, Portalegre is an important provincial centre in the Upper Alentejo. The town became prosperous with the foundation of silk mills in the 17th century, and many fine houses from this period can still be seen. A tapestry-weaving factory is situated in the former Jesuit monastery, and the ramparts surrounding the original town are still largely intact. Portalegre offers a good selection of places to stay.

Portimão

Portimão, 20 km east of Lagos, is the Algarve's most picturesque and busiest fishing port. You get a very good view of the harbour and the brightly-painted fishing boats from the bridge over the River Arade, as you come into the town from the east. Portimão is also quite an important boat-building and fish-canning centre. Not in itself a resort, it is the base for the large and important tourist developments at Penina and Torralta to the west, and serves also the well-established resort of Praia da Rocha (south), and the growing holiday centre of Praia dos Tres Irmãos.

Penina is noted for its golf courses, its vast and luxurious Golf Hotel, casino, riding, tennis, and other amenities. Strictly speaking, its location should be given as Montes de Alvor. Torralta, at Alvor nearer the coast, already possesses huge numbers of apartments and villas, together with restaurants, tennis, and riding. The Praia dos Tres Irmãos lies close to Torralta. For Praia da Rocha see below.

Póvoa de Varzim

Lying beside a lovely beach of fine white sand about 30 km north of Oporto, Póvoa de Varzim is a well-established resort that has grown up beside an ancient fishing port. The fishermen's quarter with its small houses lies to the south, and the beach opposite it is almost as busy and colourful as the shore at Nazaré. One main difference is that the men wear white woollen jerseys embroidered in varied colours. Collecting seaweed for use as fertiliser is also a regular foreshore occupation. Apart from its fine beach, the resort district offers underwater fishing, sea-fishing, and a host of amenities including bullfighting, and a casino.

Praia da Luz See Lagos.

Praia da Our See Albufeira.

Praia da Rocha

Though administratively a suburb of Portimão, Praia da Rocha is one of the Algarve's best-known resorts whose fine, sandy beach, punctuated by tall clumps of eroded rocks, has appeared on innumerable posters. The town, all newly-built and still expanding, stands on low cliffs overlooking the beach. It provides a full range of holiday facilities.

Quarteira

Quarteira is a small Algarve fishing port, half-way between Albufeira and Faro. The centre of a major holiday area, it serves, together with Almancil, 7 km inland, as a base for three of the Algarve's largest and most important holiday and residential developments—Vilamoura, Vale de Lobo, and Quinta do Lago. All are exceptionally luxurious and laid out among vast expanses of gently rolling land, liberally sprinkled with umbrella pines. All three have golf courses, tennis courts, riding centres, and, of course, good swimming. In addition, Vale de Lobo boasts an extremely luxurious hotel. Vilamoura has the Algarve's first specially-designed marina, 2 golf courses, a casino, several hotels, and much else.

Queluz

Queluz, 13 km west of Lisbon, possesses a former royal palace built between 1758 and 1794 in imitation of Versailles. The throne room is particularly sumptuous, and one of the guardrooms contains azulejos depicting Chinese and Brazilian scenes. The very attractive gardens were laid out in 1762 in imitation of Le Nôtre's style (Versailles's gardens and the original St James's Park in London).

Quinta do Lago See Quarteira.

Sagres

Sagres today is an unimportant village at the extreme western end of the Algarve coast. Its fame comes from the bare, rock-covered bleak promontory, hundreds of metres above sea level, surrounded by sheer drops into the unresting Atlantic which stretches south-west from the village. It was here that Prince Henry established his epoch-making School of Navigation (see p. 31). There is little to see—just the tiny chapel of Our Lady of Grace (Nossa Senhora das Graças), and a low building that has been turned into a Youth Hostel, where a film about Prince Henry and the great discoveries is shown each day (English version 15.30). The windswept site is enormously impressive, with its view of the cliff-lined bay.

Cape St Vincent itself, only 6 km from Sagres, can also be visited from the village. Its associations with British naval history—to say nothing of Robert Browning's poem 'Oh to be in England now that April's there'—make it almost a place of pilgrimage for Britons.

Salema See Lagos.

Santarém

Santarém stands on a hill beside the River Tagus, overlooking the vast plain of the Ribatejo province, whose capital it is. Its name is derived from St Irene, a 7th-century nun. Her body floated ashore at this point after she had been murdered by a monk whose advances she had rejected. The town's recapture from the Moors in 1147 was a vital step in the Christian reconquest of Portugal.

Santarém has been built on a steep hill. Its winding streets are lined with pantiled and tile-hung houses, and its many squares provide an air of spaciousness. It is famous for bullfighting, the Ribatejo bulls being considered Portugal's best.

The city's main sights include the vast square known as the Campo de Sá de Bandeira.

There are several interesting churches in the town.

An archaeological museum with exhibits going back to Moorish times is also housed in a former church, that of São João de Alporão.

Santarém is a possible touring base although it possesses only modest hotels.

Santiago de Cacém

Some 140 km south of Lisbon on the main road to Lagos, Santiago do Cacém is a small town dominated by a 13th-century castle built by the Templars. Sines, one of Portugal's best sea-fishing bases, lies 17 km south-west. Santiago's pousada provides rather simpler accommodation than most state inns.

São Bras de Alportel

São Bras is a small inland Algarve town in the hills 17 km north of Faro on the main road to Lisbon. A pousada with fine views stretching down to the coast stands on the town's highest point.

Sesimbra

Sesimbra is a tiny fishing port 60 km south of Lisbon and about 30 west of Setúbal. It is also something of an international holiday resort, with one four-star hotel and other, more modest accommodation. Sesimbra is famous chiefly for its sea-fishing, its sandy

beach, and its fishermen's Festival of Our Lady of the Wounds
which takes place every May 3rd-5th, and includes processions,
fireworks, and other festivities.

Setúbal

Setúbal, at the other end of the Serra de Arrábida from Sesimbra,
lies on the enormously broad Sado estuary. Like Faro in the
Algarve, it is famous for the breeding of young oysters.
Thousands of tons are shipped every year to France. It is an
important industrial area with activities that include cement
manufacture, chemicals, car and lorry assembly, and fish canning.
Setúbal is also a notable fishing centre with a fleet of some 2000
boats, a major port—Portugal's third busiest—and a flourishing
resort. It is known, too, for its muscatel wine and its marmalade.
The town has been important for many centuries—the remains of
Roman villas can be visited on the Troia promontory across the
Sado—and the old centre, with its narrow alleys and small houses,
forms a striking contrast to the modern town's broad avenues and
spacious houses.

St Philip's Castle, west of the town, was built in 1590 during the
Spanish occupation, partly to intimidate the people of Setúbal and
partly to prevent an English invasion. The Church of Jesus (Igreja
de Jesus), off the broad Avenida 22 de Dezembro running north-
wards from the old town's western edge, was built of Arrábida
marble in 1491 and contains the earliest examples of Manueline
decoration in all Portugal. The chancel pillars and vaulting are
outstanding. Adjoining the church, the Municipal Museum
(Museu da Cidade) displays a fine collection of 15th and 16th-
century Portuguese paintings in the upper galleries, with 16th-
century azulejos decorated in Moorish-style geometric designs
downstairs.

Setúbal offers tennis, riding, boat excursions, and sea-fishing as
well as first-rate swimming. The beaches on the Troia promontory
are of particularly fine sand. You reach them by a 20-minute ferry
trip from the quay beside the yacht harbour (doca de recreio).

Silves

Once an important port and the capital of the region during the
Moorish occupation, when it was known as Xelb, Silves lies a little
inland towards the Algarve's western end. In the course of
centuries the River Arade, on which the town stands, has silted up
so that only tiny vessels can reach it by water today. At the height
of its fame and prosperity, however, during the 11th and 12th
centuries, Xelb was said to rival even Lisbon in its magnificence.
The sandstone walls of the vast Moorish castle rising above the

town still recall something of those days of glory. When it was captured by Crusaders and Portuguese, in 1244, this fortress could hold 30,000 men. The vast cistern that guaranteed them a whole year's water supply can still be seen. From the battlements there is a fine view over the hills, woods, and cork factories of the surrounding region. Silves' former Cathedral, built soon after the town was captured by the Crusaders, is simple but beautiful. The many tombs that you see in it are said to contain Crusaders killed in the attack on the town.

Sines See Santiago da Cacém.

Sintra

The name Sintra indicates two interlinked attractions—the extraordinary granite Serra de Sintra, with its wild scenery and many fascinating old buildings, and the little town of Sintra containing the elegant small palace that was a favourite residence of Portugal's kings for some 600 years. The town lies on the northern slopes of the miniature mountain range, about 30 km north-west of Lisbon. The little Serra de Sintra, roughly 10 km long and 5 wide, rising to a maximum height of 530 m (1730 feet), possesses an extraordinary richness and grandeur, due partly to the region's granite ruggedness and partly to its seemingly contradictory dense green vegetation. Every sort of tree and shrub found in northern, Mediterranean, and tropical regions grows wild here—and to a tremendous size. The eucalyptus trees, in particular, are enormously tall. In several places great forests of them sweep down steep hillsides incongruously carpeted with the thick bracken associated with northern climates. Not surprisingly, the Serra de Sintra's beauty has been sung by many poets, including Southey and Byron. In sordid technical terms the scenery is simply a result of the conjunction of Mediterranean-region warmth with rain-carrying clouds coming in from the Atlantic and dropping their moisture on the granite mountain.

A picturesque circular drive from Sintra takes you out past the house called Seteais (Seven Sighs)—where Wellington signed an armistice permitting the French to leave Portugal unharmed in 1808, to the great disappointment of the Portuguese—and then to the little wine town of Colares, and to Almocageme 5 km beyond. On the way you can visit the beautifully landscaped Monserrate Park surrounding a neo-Oriental 18th-century palace. At Almocageme you turn back towards Sintra by the southern road. A turning takes you to a long-deserted Capuchin monastery (Convento dos Capuchos) where you can see the monks' tiny cells cut into the rock and lined with cork. Another steep, rough lane leads up to tiny Peninha chapel, whose interior is lined with 17th-century azulejos. It stands on a hilltop 486 m (almost 1600 feet) above the sea, with magnificent views that include the huge sandy Guincho beach to the south-west. Later you come to the ruins of an ancient Moorish castle spread over several rocky hilltops—you have to walk up from a conveniently-sited car park—with Pena Palace on a neighbouring peak, and its superb vast park containing all manner of rare trees. The Palace itself was built in the 19th century, round a 16th-century monastery, in a jumble of styles. Beyond Pena you tumble steeply back into Sintra down a series of sharp hairpin bends, passing on the way the Estalagem dos Cavaleiros, where Byron planned *Childe Harold*. This whole route, efficiently signposted throughout, takes you up and down densely forested steep mountainsides with continuously changing magnificent views. If you have time for nothing else in Portugal, you should make this tour. A short extension from Colares allows you to visit the beautiful seaside village of Azenhas do Mar, perched on a cliffside.

In Sintra town the chief attraction is the Royal Palace (Paço Real). The building was begun in the 14th century and is dominated by two extraordinarily tall conical chimneys. Every period since the Palace's foundations were laid has left its mark: there are Moorish and Manueline windows, 16th and 17th-century azulejos, a fine Armoury, and a Reading Room whose ceiling is painted with magpies—a king's gibe at gossiping court ladies.

A quick look at Sintra is sometimes included in coach tours from Lisbon that take in also Estoril and Cascais, or with trips from the two latter resorts that go much further afield. But the region deserves much more time than this.

Tavira

Tavira is an ancient town standing a few kilometres from the coast near the Algarve's border with Spain. Its bridge over the River Gilão in the town centre stands on Roman foundations. The ramparts of the fortress above the town go back to Moorish times and allow the visitor to see the fine view over the town. The church of St Mary of the Castle (Santa Maria do Castelo) was originally a mosque. St Paul's Church contains Dutch tiles imported into Portugal in the earliest days of the azulejos craze.

Tavira today is a typically quiet Algarve town. In July and August it becomes a busy centre for tunny fishing, carried out with the aid of huge nets in which the fish, weighing up to a quarter of a tonne each, are trapped and then killed by hand.

Tomar

The little town of Tomar lies along the banks of the River Nabão, 20 km east of Fátima and about 40 from Batalha. It is a quiet spot, with narrow streets and shaded gardens, dominated by a small wooded hill. On the summit of the hill 12th-century fortifications enclose the beautiful buildings that were formerly the headquarters of the Order of Christ.

In 1160 a Grand Master of the Knights Templar built a fortified castle on the hilltop. In 1314, however, the Templars were disbanded at the Pope's request and, a few years later, King Dinis I created the purely Portuguese Order of Christ. They took over the castle at Tomar and in the centuries that followed added considerably to the Templars' structure, making it one of Portugal's outstanding buildings.

Apart from the fortification walls, the monastery's oldest part is the Templars' Rotunda (Charola), built in the 12th century on the model of the Church of the Holy Sepulchre that still stands in Jerusalem's Old City. In shape it is a 16-sided polygon, containing a two-storeyed octagonal structure supported on columns and topped by a cupola. The paintings and coloured statues in this striking building date from the 16th century.

The church nave which the Order of Christ built onto the Rotunda's western side is notable chiefly for its extraordinarily exuberant Manueline design, though the doorway into the church is reminiscent of the Plateresque style seen at its best in Salamanca and other Spanish cities (see p. 34). The nave's west end opens directly onto the Renaissance Santa Barbara cloisters, and a spiral staircase near the doorway leads to the upper gallery and to the window considered the most astonishing example of Manueline ornateness in all Portugal. Ropes, carved in stone like all the rest of the window, 'moor' it to neighbouring windows. A sea-captain's bust supports the roots of a cork oak, out of which climb two elaborate masts. Seaweed, cork, anchor chains, and cables are included elsewhere in the design, and the whole thing is topped by the cross of the Order of Christ.

Though the Convent of Christ overshadows everything else in Tomar, the town contains also an interesting 15th-century synagogue, a lovely little Renaissance church (Nossa Senhora da Conceicão), and other charming old buildings.

Tomar's accommodation includes a four-star hotel, a comfortable estalagem and a good campsite.

Torralta See Portimão.

Torres Vedras

Torres Vedras is a lively small town about 70 km north of Lisbon on the road to Obidos, Alcobaça, and Batalha. Today mainly a commercial centre, it was the key point at the northern end of the fortifications constructed by Wellington in 1810. Stretching all the way to Vila Franca de Xira, the 'Lines of Torres Vedras' secured all the land to the south between the Tagus and the sea, and played a vital part in the eventual French withdrawal. An obelisk erected by the town council in 1964 in a delightful small garden in the main square commemorates Portuguese-British cooperation and the 150th anniversary of the joint victory. The restaurant, O Barrete Preto in Rua Paiva da Andrada, can be recommended for its excellent Portuguese cooking and good service at reasonable prices.

Vale de Lobo See Quarteira.

Viana do Castelo

Stretched along the River Lima's northern bank just before it joins the sea about 70 km north of Oporto lies Viana do Castelo, a lovely old town as well as a busy modern industrial centre, fishing port, and holiday resort. A magnificent sandy beach runs north-ward along the coast west of the town.

In early medieval days Viana was just another little fishing village. After the great voyages of discovery, however, it became enormously prosperous, not only because of the Newfoundland fisheries but also through its trade with the Hanseatic cities of northern Europe. After a period of decline in the 19th century it is again prospering, thanks to deep-sea fishing, and to its metal-works, ceramics, and boat-building. It is famous also for its handicrafts, and for the outstandingly picturesque Romaria of Our Lady of the Agony (Nossa Senhora da Agonia), held every year in the 3rd week of August and lasting 3 days, the centre point of which is the charming little baroque chapel of the same name. Celebrations include folk-dancing, bullfights, concerts, a cattle fair, and an evening festival of boats and music on the river.

The old town centre, roughly rectangular in shape, contains very attractive narrow streets lined with old houses dating largely from the days of the town's great prosperity. In the Praça da Republica, the former town hall, now the Turismo office, has retained its elaborate 16th-century façade. It looks out onto a fountain of the same date. The Misericord church (1714) with its striking azulejos, and hospice (1589) on the old town hall's northern side are both elegant buildings. The Parish Church south of the town hall is mainly 14th and 15th-century, though the towers are older.

Monastery of Santa Luzia, overlooking the River Lima

Another excellent collection of 18th-century azulejos can be seen in the Municipal Museum (Museu da Cidade) in Rua Manuel Esprequeira. Pleasant public gardens slope down to the river on the town-hall side. The beach area lies to the west.

Viana is a first-rate base from which to combine enjoyment of the beach with car excursions into the lovely Minho province.

Vila do Conde

Shuttle lace has made the quiet coast resort of Vila do Conde well-known in Portugal, though it has also a few small industries. Facilities include a casino. The town lies 12 km north of Oporto, adjacent to Póvoa de Varzim. Its St Clare Convent (Mosteiro de Santa Clara) includes a 14th-century church, built originally in fortress style and containing some fine tombs. The Parish Church, also fortified, dates from the 16th century and has good Plateresque reliefs. Vila do Conde is at its liveliest during the annual Lacemakers' Festival (June 21st-24th), culminating in a grand procession on the night of St John the Baptist's Day (June 24th).

Vila Franca de Xira

An industrial town noted also for its bullfights, bulls, and traditional festivals, Vila Franca lies on the Tagus's western bank at the end of a 30-km motorway running north from Lisbon. During the Red Waistcoat (Colete Encarnado) festival in July, bulls run loose in the streets, as at Pamplona in Spain, and there are colourful processions, bullfights, music, and open-air picnics.

Vilamoura See Quarteira.

Vila Real

Vila Real is a sizeable provincial centre in Trás-os-Montes on the picturesque N2 road running north into Spain. It contains a large number of 16th to 18th-century patrician houses and is noted for the black pottery made in the region. Large quantities are brought into the town for sale at St Peter's Fair on June 29th. Vila Real boasts also a motor racing track and is a good centre from which to explore both Trás-os-Montes (see p. 42) and the Douro valley.

The Mateus estate, where the famous Mateus rosé is produced, lies about 4 km south-west. It includes a stately 18th-century residence and a garden with a lake, as well as the vineyards. There is an admission charge.

Vila Real de Santo António

Vila Real de Santo António stands on the broad Guadiana's western bank about 3 km from the sea, facing the Spanish town of Ayamonte across the river. It was built in 1774 by the Marquis of Pombal, and laid out by him in the same style as the Baixa and other parts of Lisbon. The town's purpose was to counterbalance both Ayamonte and the over-independent fishing community at nearby Monte Gordo. Today Vila Real is one of the Algarve's largest fishing and commercial centres. Its fine straight streets and elegant houses are very attractive, and it is within easy reach of the vast beach and holiday facilities at Monte Gordo.

Vila Viçosa

Vila Viçosa, 18 km from Estremoz and 35 from Elvas, is a quiet little town which today lives by its handicrafts and its history. From the 15th century until 1910 it was the chief seat of the Dukes of Bragança, whose magnificent palace is the town's chief attraction—an enormous building containing much attractive 16th, 17th, and 18th-century architecture. The old town's ramparts and castle are also worth seeing. A vast 2000-hectare (5000-acre) park, immediately north of the town, was formerly the Duke's hunting ground.

Viseu

Viseu's modern importance comes from the fact that it is the chief centre of the Dao wine-producing area. It is a sizeable provincial administrative town noted also for its handicrafts (especially lace, carpets, and black pottery). It lies 110 km south of Vila Real on the N2 leading to Coimbra and Lisbon. The old town centre is a typical tangle of narrow medieval streets, containing also a number of fine houses rather later in date. Part of the original fortifications still exist, including the stately Porta do Soar. The Cathedral (mostly 16th to 18th-century) with its 16th-century cloisters, the Cathedral Square, and the Baroque Misericord Church are among the town's notable buildings. In the 16th century Viseu rivalled Lisbon as a centre of painting, and works of that period, together with much other material of interest to art-lovers, can be seen in the Grão Vasco Museum, housed in an elegant 16th to 18th-century mansion. Viseu is quite well provided with hotels.

More Fortresses and Fortified Towns

Almourol Castle A romantic-looking fortress on a tiny island in the River Tagus, about 121 km from Lisbon.

Castel Branco Now the capital of Beira Baixa province but formerly a fortress town guarding the frontier with Spain. Although most of its ancient monuments have been destroyed, the town is still interesting, and the gardens of the former Bishop's Palace particularly beautiful.

Castelo de Vide Close to the Spanish frontier on the main road (N118) from Santarém, it has retained its 12th-century castle and ancient Jewish quarter.

Evoramonte A tiny town between Evora and Estremoz, dominated by the castle—Roman, Moorish, and medieval—on the top of the hill.

Marvão A lovely medieval town near the Spanish border, on the Santarém road; 22 km from Portalegre and 8 km from Castelo de Vide on Route N118.

A Pronunciation Guide

Stress

In words ending with a vowel, *m*, *n*, or *s*, the stress is on the next to last syllable. Words ending in consonants other than the above are stressed on the last syllable. Stresses other than these are marked with an accent.

Vowels

The vowel sound is altered according to whether it is in a stressed or unstressed syllable.

a	as in f*a*ther	—in a stressed syllable, or *á*, sometimes in an unstressed syllable, too
	as in *a*bout	—in an unstressed syllable, or *â*
e	as in s*e*t	—in most stressed syllables, or *é*
	as in f*a*te	—in certain stressed syllables, or *ê*
	almost silent	—in an unstressed syllable, especially when final
i	as in mach*i*ne—	
o	as in n*o*rth	—in a stressed syllable, *ó*, or followed by *l*+consonant
	as in n*o*te	—in a stressed syllable, *ô* (the commonest sound)
	as in b*oo*t	—in an unstressed syllable
u	as in b*oo*t	—in a stressed syllable
	as in f*oo*t	—in an unstressed syllable

Consonants

The consonant is pronounced differently according to whether its position in a word or syllable is initial, medial, or final.

b	silent when final	
c	as in *c*at	
	before *e* or *i*, or *ç*, as in *s*at	
ch	as in *sh*oe	
d	as in *d*og—initially before vowels	
	medially after *l*, *n*, *r*	
	as in *th*ough—in all other cases	
g	as in *g*ot	
	before *e* or *i* as in a*z*ure	
gu	as in *g*ot	
h	always silent	
j	as in a*z*ure	
m	silent when final or before consonants (except *b* or *p*), but nazalises the preceding vowel	
n	silent when final or before *d*, *t*, *k*, *g*, but nazalises the preceding vowel	
qu	as in *qu*een	
	before *e* or *i* as in *c*at	
r	as in ve*r*y—between vowels, medially or finally in a syllable	
r	trilled—beginning of syllable, or doubled	
s	as in *s*un—initially, after consonants, or doubled	
	as in pre*s*ent—between vowels	
	as in *sh*oe—finally, or before consonants *p*, *k*, *t*, *f*	
	as in plea*s*ure—before consonants other than the above	
x	as in *sh*oe—in most positions	
	as in *s*o—also between vowels	
	as in *z*eal—before a vowel, or in prefix *ex*-	
z	as in *z*ebra—initially, and medially	
	as in *sh*all—finally	

Vocabulary

Everyday Expressions

Mr.	*Senhor*
Mrs.	*Senhora*
Miss	*Menina*
Please	*Por favor*
Thank you	*Obrigado*
Good morning	*Bom dia*
Good day	*Bom dia*
Good afternoon	*Boa tarde*
Good evening (until sunset)	*Boa tarde*
Good night (after sunset)	*Boa noite*
Good-bye	*Adeus*
Yes	*Sim*
No	*Não*
How do you do?	*Como está?*
Very well, and you?	*Muito bem, e Você?*
Excuse me (pardon me)	*Desculpe*
Excuse me (with your permission)	*Com licença*
I am English	*Sou inglês (a)*
Do you speak English?	*Fala inglês?*
I cannot speak Portuguese	*Não falo português*
I want . . .	*Quero . . .*
Come in	*Entre*
That's all right	*Está bem*
You are most kind	*O senhor* } *é muito amável* *A senhora*
Never mind	*Não tem importância*
Don't worry	*Não se preocupe*
Am I disturbing you?	*Estou a incomodar?*
May I introduce . . .	*Permite-me apresentar . . .*
I don't mind	*Não me importo*
I don't think so	*Não creio*
I am very grateful to you	*Estou-lhe muito agradecido*
What is this (that)?	*O que é isto (aquilo)?*
Like this (that)	*Como isto (aquilo)*
This (that) side	*Este (aquele) lado*
It is (was) wonderful	*É (foi) maravilhoso*
Will this (that) do?	*Serve isto (isso)?*
I agree	*Estou de acordo*
Help yourself	*Sirva-se*
What is the time?	*Que horas são?*

In difficulty

Can you help me?	*Pode ajudar-me?*
I am looking for . . .	*Estou à procura . . .*
Can you direct me to . . .?	*Pode dizer-me como chegar a . . .?*
I am lost	*Estou perdido*
Where is the British Consulate?	*Onde é o Consulado Britânico?*
Speak slowly	*Fale devagar*
I am hungry (thirsty)	*Tenho fome (sede)*
I am busy (tired)	*Estou ocupado (cansado)*
I am sorry	*Sinto muito. Desculpe*
What a pity!	*Que pena!*
What do you want?	*O que deseja?*
What do you mean?	*Que quer o senhor (a) dizer?*
I do not know	*Não sei*

I do not understand	*Não compreendo*
I do not agree	*Não estou de acordo*
I do not like it	*Não gosto disso*
I must go now	*Tenho que ir embora*
It is forbidden	*Prolbe-se*
It is urgent	*É urgente*
Hurry up!	*Depressa!*
Be careful!	*Cuidado!*
Look out!	*Atenção!*
Be quiet!	*Esteja calado (a)!*
Leave me alone!	*Deixe-me!*
I shall call a policeman	*Chamarei um policia*
Help!	*Socorro!*

after	*depois*	more	*mais*
against	*contra*	much	*muito*
agreed	*de acordo*	near	*perto*
all	*todo*	next	*próximo*
almost	*quase*	now	*agora*
among	*entre*	not	*não*
before	*antes que*	okay	*está bem*
behind	*atrás*	on	*sôbre*
below	*abaixo de*	outside	*por fora* ·
beside	*ao lado de*	over	*acima de*
between	*entre*	perhaps	*talvez*
cold	*frio*	quick	*rápido*
downstairs	*lá embaixo*	right	*direito*
elsewhere	*parte noutra*	slow	*devagar*
enough	*bastante*	somebody	*alguém*
everybody	*todos*	something	*alguma coisa*
everything	*tudo*	that	*aquilo*
everywhere	*em toda a parte*	there	*ali*
except	*excepto*	these	*estes, estas*
far	*distante*	this	*este, esta*
for	*por, para*	those	*aqueles*
here	*aqui*	through	*através*
hot	*quente*	too	*também*
in	*em*	towards	*para*
in front of	*em frente de*	until	*até*
inside	*por dentro*	upstairs	*em cima*
last	*último*	very	*muito*
left	*esquerdo*	welcome	*bem-vindo*
less	*menos*	when	*quando*
listen	*escutar*	where	*onde*
little	*pequeno*	why	*porquê*
look	*olhar*	without	*sem*
many	*muitos*		

Accommodation

I have reserved a room (two rooms)	*Reservei um (dois) quarto(s)*
I wish to stay for . . .	*Quero ficar até . . . .*
I do not want meals	*Não quero refeições*
I shall not be here for lunch	*Não estarei para o almoço*
May I take a packed lunch?	*Posso ter um piquenique?*
I want breakfast only	*Só quero pequeno almoço*
I want a room with one bed (two beds, a double bed)	*Quero um quarto com uma cama (duas camas, cama de casal)*

I want a room with a private bathroom	*Quero um quarto com banho privativo*
I am on a diet	*Estou em regime de dieta*
I cannot eat . . .	*Não posso comer . . .*
What are your charges, including (excluding) meals?	*Quais são os preços, com (sem) comida?*
What time is breakfast (lunch, dinner, tea)?	*A que horas è o pequeno almoço (o almoço, o jantar, o chá)?*
I should like something cheaper	*Quero uma coisa mais baratà*
Have you a room with a better view?	*Tem um quarto com melhor vista?*
I want to leave early tomorrow	*Quero ir-me embora amanhã cedo*
Wake me at . . .	*Desperte-me às . . . horas*
Can I have my clothes pressed?	*Podem passar a minha roupa?*
Can I have my shoes cleaned?	*Podem engraxar os meus sapatos?*
Can I drink the water from the tap?	*Posso beber a àgua da torneira?*
I want a hot bath	*Quero um banho quente*
Is there a plug for my electric razor?	*Hà uma tomada para a minha màquina de barbear?*
What is the voltage?	*Qual è a voltagem?*
I have some things to be washed	*Tenho roupa para lavar*
Will you get this mended?	*Pode mandar reparar isto?*
When will they be ready?	*Quando estarão prontos?*
When does the hotel close?	*Quando fecha o hotel?*
I shall be very late	*Voltarei muito tarde*
May I have a key?	*Pode dar-me uma chave?*
Is there a night porter?	*Hà um porteiro de noite?*
Forward my mail to this address	*Faça o favor de remeter o meu correio para este endereço*

armchair	*a poltrona*	coat-hanger	*o cabide*
bath	*o banho*	cook	*o cozinheiro*
bathroom	*o quarto de banho*	curtain	*a cortina*
bed	*a cama*	dining-room	*a sala de jantar*
bedroom	*o quarto de dormir*	eiderdown	*o edredon*
bedroom, single	*o quarto para uma pessoa*	floor (storey)	*o andar*
		hotel	*o hotel*
double	*o quarto para duas pessoas*	hotel-keeper	*o recepcionista*
		hot-water bottle	*a botija*
with twin beds	*o quarto com duas camas*	key	*a chave*
		large	*grande*
with a double bed	*o quarto com cama de casal*	larger	*maior*
		lavatory	*a toilette*
bell	*a campainha*	lift	*o elevador*
better	*melhor*	manager	*o gerente*
bill	*a conta*	mattress	*o colchão*
blanket	*o cobertor*	office	*o escritorio*
blind	*a cortina*	pillow	*a almofada*
boarding-house	*a pensão*	plug (electric)	*a tomada*
board (full)	*a pensão completa*	porter	*o porteiro*
		proprietor	*o proprietário*
board (half)	*meia-pensão*	quiet	*sossegado*
bulb (electric light)	*a lâmpada*	quieter	*mais sossegado*
		radiator	*o radiador*
chair	*a cadeira*	reading-lamp	*o candeeiro*
chambermaid	*a empregada de quarto*	sheet	*o lençol*
		shower	*o chuveiro*

shutter	o postigo .	table	a mesa
sitting-room	a sala de extar	tap	a torneira
small	pequeno	terrace	o terraço
smaller	mais pequeno	towel	a toalha
soap	o sabonete	wardrobe	o guarda-roupa
staircase	as escadas	washbasin	o lavatório
switch (light)	o interruptor da luz	window	a janela

Beach and Bathing

Where is the beach?	Onde é a praia?
Where can I bathe?	Onde posso banhar-me?
Is it safe to swim here?	Posso banhar-me aqui sem perigo?
Is it deep or shallow?	É funda ou não a água?
Is the beach sandy or pebbly?	A praia é arenosa ou pedregosa?
I want to hire a . . .	Quero alugar um . . .
Where can I change?	Onde posso mudar-me?
I cannot swim very well	Não sei nadar muito bem
Help! Someone is drowning!	Socorro! Afoga-se alguém!
Can I go underwater swimming here?	Posso nadar debaixo de água aqui?
Bathing prohibited	É proibido tomar banho

air mattress	a colchão pneumática	lifebelt	o cinto de salvação
bathe	o banho	lighthouse	o farol
bathing cap	a touca de banho	mask	a máscara
bathing costume	o fato de banho	octopus	o polvo
bathing hat	a touca de banho	pebble	o calhau
beach	a praia	raft	a jangada
beach umbrella	o guarda-sol	rock	a rocha
boat	o barco	rowing-boat	o barco a remos
buoy	a bóia	sand	a areia
canoe	a canoa	sea	o mar
cliff	o penhasco	shark	o tubarão
coast	a costa	shell	a concha
crab	o caranguejo	snorkel tube	o tubo para respiração
current	a corrente	speargun	a espingarda de arpão
danger	o perigo		
deckchair	a cadeira de lona	sun	o sol
dive, to	mergulhar	sunshade	o toldo
fish, to	pescar	surf board	a tábua de surf
flippers	as nadadeiras	tide	a maré
harpoon	o arpão	towel	a toalha
jelly-fish	a alforreca		
knife	a faca		

Camping

Where does this road lead?	Onde vai dar este caminho?
How far is it to . . .?	A que distância fica . . .?
What is the name of this place?	Como é que se chama este lugar?
Is there a Youth Hostel near here?	Há um albergue da juventude perto?
Can we cut across country?	Podemos atravessar o campo?
We are lost	Perdemos o caminho
We are looking for a camping site	Estamos à procura dum parque de campismo
May we light a fire?	Podemos fazer uma fogueira?
Where is the toilet (washroom)?	Onde é a toilette (lavatorio)?

I should like to hire a bicycle
Where can I buy methylated spirit (paraffin)?

Quero alugar uma bicicleta
Onde posso comprar alcóol desnaturado (parafina)?

bottle opener	*o saca-rolhas*	path	*o caminho*
bucket	*o balde*	penknife	*o canivete*
camp	*acampamento*	picnic	*o piquenique*
camping equipment	*o equipamento de campismo*	river	*o rio*
		road	*a estrada*
camping site	*o parque de campismo*	rope	*a corda*
		rubbish	*o lixo*
candle	*a vela*	sandwich	*a sanduíche*
caravan	*a roulotte*	saucepan	*a panela*
country	*o campo*	sleeping-bag	*o saco de dormir*
field	*o prado*	store	*a loja*
ground sheet	*o lençol impermeável*	tent	*a barraca*
		tent peg	*a estaca para barraca*
haversack	*o farnel*		
hitch-hike	*pedir boleia*	thermos	*o termos*
hill	*a colina*	tin opener	*o abre latas*
inn	*a estalagem*	torch	*a pilha*
lake	*o lago*	waterproof	*o impermeável*
matches	*os fósforos*	wood	*a lenha*
mountain	*a montanha*		

Church

Where is a Roman Catholic church (Protestant church, synagogue, mosque)?
At what time are the services held?
Is there an English-speaking priest?

Onde há uma igreja católica (igreja protestante, sinagoga, mesquita)?
A que horas têm oficios religiosos?
Há um padre que fale inglês?

Colours

black	*preto*	orange	*côr de laranja*
blue	*azul*	pink	*côr-de-rosa*
brown	*castanho*	purple	*purpura*
cream	*creme*	red	*vermelho*
crimson	*carmesim*	scarlet	*escarlate*
fawn	*beige*	silver	*prateado*
gold	*dourado*	violet	*violeta*
green	*verde*	white	*branco*
grey	*cinzento*	yellow	*amarelo*

Days of the Week

Sunday	*domingo*	Thursday	*quinta-feira*
Monday	*segunda-feira*	Friday	*sexta-feira*
Tuesday	*terça-feira*	Saturday	*sábado*
Wednesday	*quarta-feira*		

Months

January	*Janeiro*	July	*Julho*
February	*Fevereiro*	August	*Agosto*
March	*Março*	September	*Setembro*
April	*Abril*	October	*Outubro*
May	*Maio*	November	*Novembro*
June	*Junho*	December	*Dezembro*

Entertainment

Where is a good (cheap) night club?

Onde há uma boîte boa (barata)?

Would you care to dance?		Gostaria de dançar?
Where can I dance?		Onde posso dançar?
What would you like to drink?		O que quer beber?

band	a banda
box	o camarote
box office	a bilheteira
casino	o casino
cinema	o cinema
cloakroom ticket	a senha do vestiário
concert hall	a sala de concêrto
dance	a baile
dance, to	dançar

dance hall	a sala de baile
entertainments	as diversões
film	o filme
gaming-room	a sala de jogo
interval	o intervalo
night club	a boîte
seat	o lugar
stage	o palco
stall	a plateia
theatre	o teatro

Food and Restaurants

Where is a good (cheap) restaurant?	Onde há um restaurante bom (barato)?
Where is a quick-service restaurant?	Onde há um restaurante de serviço rápido?
Where is a good restaurant for seafood?	Onde há um bom restaurante para mariscos?
Where is a good restaurant for dishes?	Onde há um bom restaurante para pratos locais?
Can we lunch here?	Podemos almoçar aqui?
I should like a table near the window	Quero uma mesa perta da janela
I only want a snack	Só quero uma refeição leve
I am in a hurry	Estou com pressa
I should like to wash my hands	Quero lavar as mãos
Have you the menu?	Tem o menú?
I like it underdone (medium) (well done)	Quero-o mal passado (meio passado) (bem passado)
A little more	Um pouco mais
That's too much	Isso é demais
I did not order this	Não pedi isto
Bring me another	Traga-me outro
This is cold	Isto está frio
I have had enough	Já tive o suficiente
May I have the bill?	Traz-me a conta?
Is the service included?	Está incluido o serviço?
Is this correct?	Está correcto?
Please check it	Faça o favor de verificá-lo
I made a mistake	Enganei-me
I'm sorry	Desculpe
Keep the change	Fique com o troco
We enjoyed the meal	Gostámos muito da refeição

ashtray	o cinzeiro
bar	o bar
bill	a conta
bottle	a garrafa
canned	enlatado
clean	limpo
cork	a rolha
cup	a chávena
dirty	sujo
fork	o garfo
fresh	fresco

glass	o copo
knife	a faca
meal	a refeição
menu, bill of fare	o menú
not clean	não está limpo
not fresh	não está fresco
plate	o prato
saucer	o pires
serviette, napkin	o guardanapo
spoon	o colher

tablecloth	a toalha de mesa	lamb	o cordeiro
teapot	o bule de chá	lemon	o limão
tip	a gorjeta	lettuce	a alface
waiter	o empregado de mesa	liver	o fígado
		lobster	a lagosta
waiter (head)	o chefe de mesa	marmalade	o doce de laranja
waiter (wine)	o empregado de mesa	melon	o melão
		mushroom	o cogumelo
waitress	a empregada de mesa	mussels	os mexilhões
		mustard	a mostarda
water-jug	o jarro	mutton	o carneiro
wine list	a lista de vinhos	oil	o azeite
food		olive oil	o azeite
apple	a maçã	onion	a cebola
apricot	o damasco	orange	a laranja
artichoke	a alcachofra	oyster	a ostra
asparagus	o espargo	pastry	a pastelaria
bacon	o toucinho	peach	o pêssego
banana	a banana	peanuts	os amendoins
beans	o feijão	pear	a pera
beef	a carne de vaca	peas	as ervilhas
biscuit	a bolacha	pepper	a pimenta
bread (white)	o pão	pickles	os pickles
bread (brown)	o pão de centeio	pineapple	o ananás
butter	a manteiga	plum	a ameixa
cabbage	a couve	pork	o porco
cake	o bolo	potato	a batata
carrot	a cenoura	prawn	o camarão
cauliflower	a couve-flor	prunes	as ameixas secas
caviare	o caviar	raisins	as passas
celery	o aipo	raspberry	a framboesa
cheese	o queijo	rice	o arroz
cherries	as cerejas	roll	o pãozinho
chicken	o frango	salad	a salada
chocolate	o chocolate	salmon	o salmão
chops	as costeletas	salt	o sal
crab	o caranguejo	sardine	a sardinha
crayfish	o caranguejo de rio	sauce	o molho
		sausage (beef)	o salami
cream	a nata	sausage (pork)	a salsicha
cucumber	o pepino	scampi	os camarões
dessert	a sobremesa	seafood	os mariscos
egg	o ovo	shrimp	o camarão
figs	os figos	snail	o caracol
fish	o peixe	sole	o linguado
fruit	a fruta	soup (clear)	o caldo
game	a caça	soup (thick)	a sopa
garlic	o alho	spinach	o espinafre
grapes	as uvas	steak	o bife
grapefruit	a toranja	strawberry	o morango
ham	o fiambre	sugar	o açúcar
honey	o mel	toast	a torrada
hors-d'oeuvres	os hors-d'oeuvres	tomato	o tomate
ice	o gelo	trout	a truta
ice-cream	o gelado	vanilla	a baunilha
jam	a compota	veal	a vitela
kidney	o rim	vegetables	os legumes
		vinegar	o vinagre

Drink

What would you like to drink?		*O que gostaria de beber?*	
What do you suggest?		*O que sugere?*	
I should like . . .		*Eu queria . . .*	
Your health!		*À sua saude!*	

alcoholic drink	*a bebida alcoólica*	mineral water	*a água mineral*
apéritif	*o aperitivo*	mug	*a caneca*
beer (light)	*a cerveja*	nip	*o trago*
beer (dark)	*a cerveja (preta)*	non-alcoholic	*sem álcool*
bottle (half)	*(meia) garrafa*	orangeade	*a laranjada*
brandy	*a aguardente*	port	*o vinho do Porto*
carafe	*o jarro*	rum	*o rum*
champagne	*a champanha*	sherry	*o xerez*
chocolate	*o chocolate*	soda water	*a soda*
cider	*a cidra*	tea (with milk)	*o chá (com leite)*
cocktail	*o cocktail*	tea (with lemon)	*o chá (de limão)*
coffee (white)	*o café com leite*	tea (without milk)	*o chá (sem leite)*
coffee (black)	*o café*		
gin	*o gin*	tonic water	*a água tónica*
glass	*o copo*	vermouth	*o vermute*
ice	*o gelo*	vodka	*a vodka*
jug	*o jarro*	water	*a água*
lager	*a cerveja dinamarquesa*	whisky	*o uisque*
		wine, dry	*o vinho seco*
lemon	*o limão*	sweet	*o vinho doce*
lemonade	*a limonada*	red	*o vinho tinto*
liqueur	*o licor*	rosé	*o vinho rosado*
milk	*o leite*	white	*o vinho branco*
milk shake	*o batido*	local	*o vinho da càsa*

Health

Send for a doctor	*Chame um médico*
It is broken	*Está quebrado*
Have you any bandages?	*Tem ligaduras?*
Do not move him (her)	*Não o (a) mova*
I am not feeling well	*Não-me sinto bem*
I have a pain here	*Tenho uma dôr aqui*
I have a headache	*Tenho uma dôr de cabeça*
I have a sore throat	*Tenho a garganta dorida*
My stomach is upset	*Tenho o estômago indispôsto*
I feel much better	*Sinto-me muito melhor*
Can you recommend a dentist?	*Pode recomendar um dentista?*
I have a toothache	*Doem-me os dentes*
I want it out	*Tire-mo*
I should like an injection	*Quero uma injeção*
You are hurting me	*Doi-me*
Can you make up this prescription?	*Pode preparar-me esta receita?*
When will it be ready?	*Quando estará pronto?*
Can you give me a remedy for . . .?	*Pode dar-me um remédio para . . .?*
For external use only	*Só para emprego exterior*
One teaspoonful (tablespoonful) in a glass of water	*Uma colher de chá (de sopa) num copo de água*

accident	*o acidente*	bite	*a picada*
ambulance	*a ambulância*	bleeding	*o sangrar*
bandage	*a ligadura*	blister	*a bolha*

boil	o furúnculo	sprain	a entorce
burn (scald)	a queimadura (escaldadura)	sting	a picada
		stomach-ache	a dor de estómago
cold	a constipação	sunburn	a queimadura de sol
constipation	a prisão de ventre		
cough	a tosse	sunstroke	a insolação
cramp	a cãibra	surgery	a sala de médico
cut	o corte	swelling	o inchaço
dangerous	perigoso	temperature	a temperatura
dentist	o dentista	toothache	a dor de dentes
diarrhoea	a diarreia	vomit	o vómito
diet	a dieta	wound	a ferida
doctor	o médico	**chemist**	
faint	o desmaio	aspirin	a aspirina
fever	o febre	contraceptive	o preservativo
filling (stopping)	a obturação	cotton-wool	o algodão em rama
gas	o gás		
hay-fever	o febre do feno	gargle	o gargarejo
headache	a dor de cabeça	gauze	o gaze
hospital	o hospital	iodine	o iôdo
illness	a doença	laxative	o laxante
indigestion	a indigestão	medicine	a medicina
injection	a injecção	powder (talcum)	o talco
insomnia	a insónia	prescription	a receita
nausea	as náuseas	quinine	o quinino
nurse	a enfermeira	sanitary towel	o pano higiênico
pain	a dor	sleeping-pill	a pilula para fazer dormir
poison	o veneno		
remedy	o remédio	smelling-salts	os sais
sick, to feel	ter náuseas, enjoado	sticking-plaster	o penso adesivo
		toilet paper	o papel higiênico
sore throat	a garganta dorida	vaseline	a vaselina

Money/Banks

Where is the nearest bank?	*Onde é o Banco mais próximo?*
May I see the manager?	*Posso falar com o Gerente?*
Will you cash this (travellers') cheque?	*Faça o favor de trocar este cheque (de viagem)?*
What is the exchange rate for the pound sterling?	*Qual é taxa de câmbio da libra esterlina?*
How much is this worth?	*Quanto vale isto?*
I should like some small change	*Quero algumas moedas*

cash, to	receber na caixa	money exchange bureau	o cambista
change	o troco		
cheque	o cheque	note	a nota
coin	a moeda	pound sterling	a libra esterlina
exchange	o câmbio	rate	a taxa
letter of credit	a carta de crédito	travellers' cheque	o cheque de viagem
money	o dinheiro		

Motoring

Do you know the road to . . .?	*Conhece o caminho para . . .?*
How far is it to . . .?	*A que distancia . . .?*
I want some petrol (oil, water)	*Quero gasolina (óleo, água)*
I need . . . litres	*Preciso de . . . litros*
Have you distilled water for my battery?	*Tem água destilada para a minha bateria?*

Check the tyre pressures	Verifique a pressão nos pneus
The pressure should be . . . in front and . . . at the back	A pressão deve ser . . . à frente e . . . atrás
Is there a breakdown service?	Há serviço de reparações?
I have had a breakdown (puncture)	Tenho uma avaria (furo)
Where can I find a mechanic?	Onde posso encontrar um mecânico?
Do you do repairs?	Fazem reparações?
I have broken . . .	Parti-quebrei . . .
This does not work	Isto não funciona
Can you do it immediately?	Pode fazer já?
How long must I wait?	Quanto tempo tenho de esperar?
Where can I park?	Onde posso estacionar?
I want to hire a car	Quero alugar um automóvel
How much an hour (a day)?	Quanto por hora (dia)?
Is there an English-speaking driver?	Há um chauffeur que fale inglês?
Go more quickly	Vá mais depressa
Do not drive so fast	Não vá tão depressa
Wait here (over there)	Espere aqui (ali)
Pick me up at . . .	Venha buscar-me às . . .
I must go back by . . .	Tenho de voltar antes das . . . horas

back axle	o eixo traseiro
bend	a curva
boot	o porta bagagens
brake	o travão
breakdown	a avaria
breakdown truck	o carro de socorro
can	a lata
car	o automóvel, o carro
car licence	a licença
caravan	a roulotte
clutch	a embraiagem
convertible	o carro descapotável
cross-roads	a encruzilhada
danger	perigo
distilled water	água destilada
drive, to	guiar, conduzir
driver	o motorista, chauffeur
driving licence	a carta de condução
exhaust	tubo de escape
garage	a garagem
gear box	a caixa de velocidades
gear lever	a alavanca de mudanças
ignition key	a chave de ignição
jack	o macaco
lever	a alavanca
lights	as luzes de tráfego

lubrication	a lubrificação
mechanic	o mecânico
motorway	a auto-estrada
narrow road	a estrada estreita
no entry	entrada proibida
no parking	estacionamento proibido
oil	o óleo
overtaking prohibited	proibido ultrapassar
parking	estacionamento
pedestrian crossing	a passagem de peões
petrol	a gasolina
petrol pump	a bomba de gasolina
radiator	o radiador
repairs	as reparações
reverse	a marcha-atrás
road blocked	estrada obstruída
road junction	cruzamento
roadworks	obras
roundabout	a rotunda
school	a escola
screw	o parafuso
screwdriver	a chave de parafusos
skid	o cruzamento
slippery surface	a superfície escorregadia
slow down	disminuir a velocidade
spanner	a chave de porcas
speed	a velocidade
speed limit	o limite de velocidade

steep hill	*colina escarpada*			two-stroke mixture	*a mistura*	
steering wheel	*o volante*			uneven road	*estrada em mau estado*	
tank	*o depósito*					
traffic lights	*os sinais luminosos*			unscrew	*desaparafusar*	
tyre	*o pneu*			wheel	*a roda*	
tyre (tubeless)	*o pneu sem câmara de ar*					

Numbers

1	*um*	16	*dezesseis*	52	*cinqüenta e dois*
2	*dois*	17	*dezessete*	60	*sessenta*
3	*três*	18	*dezoito*	61	*sessenta e um*
4	*quatro*	19	*dezenove*	62	*sessenta e dois*
5	*cinco*	20	*vinte*	70	*setenta*
6	*seis*	21	*vinte e um*	71	*setenta e um*
7	*sete*	22	*vinte e dois*	72	*setenta e dois*
8	*oito*	30	*trinta*	80	*oitenta*
9	*nove*	31	*trinta e um*	81	*oitenta e um*
10	*dez*	32	*trinta e dois*	82	*oitenta e dois*
11	*onze*	40	*quarenta*	90	*noventa*
12	*doze*	41	*quarenta e um*	91	*noventa e um*
13	*treze*	42	*quarenta e dois*	92	*noventa e dois*
14	*quatorze*	50	*cinqüenta*	100	*cento*
15	*quinze*	51	*cinqüenta e um*		

Photography

I want a black and white (colour) film for this camera — *Quero um filme branco e prêto (em côr) para esta máquina*

Have you any fast film? — *Tem filme rápido?*

Will you load my camera? — *Faça o favor de carregar a máquina?*

Will you develop and print this film? — *Faça o favor de revelar e imprimir este filme?*

I want one (two, three, etc.) print(s) of each — *Quero um (dois, três) positivo(s) de cada*

When will they be ready? — *Quando estarão prontos?*

I must have them by . . . — *Quero-os antes do dia . . .*

camera	*a máquina fotográfica*	filter	*o filtro*
		lens	*a lente*
cine camera	*a máquina cine*	lens-hood	*a protecção da lente*
colour	*a côr*		
develop, to	*revelar*	negative	*o negativo*
enlargement	*a ampliação*	print	*o positivo*
exposure meter	*o fotómetro*	range-finder	*o telémetro*
film	*o filme*	shutter	*o obturador*
film winder	*o passador de filme*	view-finder	*o visor*

Post Office

Where is the nearest post office? — *Onde é Correio mais próximo?*

Give me a stamp(s) for this (these) letter(s) — *Dê-me selo(s) para esta (estas) carta(s)*

I want to express this letter — *Quero mandar esta carta expressa*

I want to register this letter — *Quero registar esta carta*

I want to send this parcel — *Quero mandar este pacote*

Have you any letters poste restante for me? — *Tem alguma carta posta restante para mim?*

I want to send a telegram to . . .	Quero mandar uma telegrama para . . .
What is the charge per word?	Quanto custa cada palavra?
I want a telephone call to England	Quero telefonar para Inglaterra
Will you get me this number?	Faça o favor de obter-me este número?
How much will it be?	Quanto custará?
You gave me the wrong number	Deu-me um número errado

call	a chamada	post card	o postal
collection	colecção	post office	o correio
directory	a lista telefónica	postal order	o vale postal
international	o vale postal	postman	o carteiro
money order	internacional	register, to	registar
letter	a carta	reply	responder
letter box	a caixa postal	stamp	o selo
number	o número	telegram	a telegrama
paid	pago	telephone	o telefone
parcel	o embrulho		

Public Notices

closed	fechado	open	aberto
cross	atravesse	pull	puxe
engaged	ocupado	push	empurre
gentlemen	homens	ring	toque
information	informações	stop, to	parar
knock	bater	toilet	toilette
ladies	senhoras	vacant	livre
no entry	passagem proibida	wait	espere
		way in	entrada
no smoking	e proibido fumar	way out	saída
occupied	ocupado		

Shopping

Where can I find a . . .?	Onde posso encontrar um . . .?
How much is . . .?	Quanto custa . . .?
I want to buy . . .	Quero comprar . . .?
Have you anything cheaper?	Tem alguma coisa mais barata?
I want something like this (that)	Quero uma coisa igual a esta
I want more (less) than that	Quero mais (menos) do que isso
I will buy this	Fico com isto
That's all	É tudo
It doesn't fit me	Não me serve
It doesn't work	Não funciona
Can you change it?	Pode trocá-lo?
Will you change it later?	Poderá ser trocado?
Can you refund my money?	Pode devolver o meu dinheiro?
My English size is . . .	O meu tamanho inglês é . . .
Will you measure me?	Quer tirar-me a medida?
May I try this on?	Posso provar isto?
Can I order one (some)?	Posso encomendar um (alguns)?
Send it to this address	Envie a esta morada
I will return later	Voltarei logo
It is too large (small)	É demasiadamente grande (pequeno)
How much each (per kilo, etc.)?	Quanto é cada (por kilo)?
Are these ripe (fresh)?	Estes são maduros (frescos)?

Repairs

I have broken (torn) this — *Parti (rasguei) isto*
Can you repair it? — *Pode remendá-lo?*
When will it be ready? — *Quando é que está pronto?*
I have to leave by . . . — *Tenho de partir antes do . . .*

Hairdressing

I want a haircut — *Quero um corte de cabelo*
I want my hair trimmed — *Quero que aparem o meu cabelo*
Don't cut it too short — *Não o corte demasiado*
I don't want any oil on my hair — *Não quero brilhantinas no cabelo*
I want a shave — *Quero barbear-me*
Trim my moustache (beard) — *Apare o meu bigode (a minha barba)*

I want this style (show design) — *Quero este estilo*
I want a shampoo and set — *Quero lavar e fazer mise*
I want a permanent wave — *Quero uma permanente*
I want a bleach (colour rinse, tint) — *Quero um descorante (uma tinta, um matiz)*
I want a manicure (pedicure) — *Quero uma manicura (pedicura)*
I want a face massage — *Quero uma massagem na cara*
Thank you. That's very nice — *Obrigado. Está muito bem*
Could I make an appointment for . . . o'clock? — *Posso vir às . . . horas?*

antiques	*antiguidades*
bag	*a carteira*
baker	*o padeiro*
ball point	*a caneta esferográfiça*
bathing suit	*o fato de banho*
bath salts	*os sais de banho*
battery	*a bateria*
belt	*o cinto*
better	*melhor*
blouse	*a blusa*
book	*o livro*
bookseller	*o livreiro*
bracelet	*a pulseira*
braces	*os suspensórios*
brassiere	*o soutien*
brooch	*o broche*
brush	*a escova*
butcher	*o carniceiro*
button	*o botão*
camera	*a máquina fotográfica*
cardigan	*a camisola*
cheap	*barato*
cheaper	*mais barato*
chemist	*o farmacêutico*
chiropodist	*o quiropodista*
cigar	*o charuto*
cigarette lighter	*o isqueiro*
cleaner	*a tinturaria*
clock	*o relógio*
clothes	*a roupa*
coat	*o casaco*
coffee	*o café*
collar	*o colarinho*
comb	*o pente*
colour rinse	*a tinta de cabelo*
cotton	*o algodão*
cosmetics	*os cosméticos*
cushion	*a almofada*
cuff-links	*os botões de punho*
cup	*a chávena*
dark	*escuro*
darker	*mais escuro*
delicatessen	*mercearia fina*
department store	*o armazém*
dictionary	*o dicionário*
disinfectant	*o desinfectante*
doll	*a boneca*
draper	*o vendedor de tecidos*
dress	*o vestido*
dry-cleaner	*a tinturaria*
ear-rings	*os brincos*
elastic	*o elástico*
envelope	*o envelope*
expensive	*caro*
fancy leather goods	*os artipos de fantasia em cabedal*
face-powder	*o pó de arroz*
fine	*fino*
finer	*mais fino*
fishmonger	*o peixeiro*

florist	a florista	pants	as cuecas
fork	o garfo	panties	as calças
fur	as peles	pen	a caneta
glasses	os óculos	pencil	o lápis
gloves	as luvas	perfume	o perfume
gold	ouro	photographer	o fotógrafo
gramophone record	o disco	pin (safety)	o alfinete de segurança
greengrocer	A loja da fruta e hortaliças	pipe	o cachimbo
		plate	o prato
grocer	o merceeiro	powder	o pó
guide book	o guia	powder compact	a caixa de pó
handbag	a carteira	powder-puff	a borla
hat	o chapéu	purse	o porta moedas
heavy	pesado	pyjamas	os pijamas
heavier	mais pesado	radio	o radio
heel	o salto	raincoat	o impermeável
high	alto	razor	a navalha
ink	a tinta	razor blade	a lâmina de barba
invisible mending	a cerzir	refill	a carga
		ribbon	a cinta
ironmonger	a loja de ferragens	rollers	os rolos
jacket	a casaco curto	sandals	as sandálias
jeweller	o joalheiro	(rope soled)	as alparcatas
label	a etiqueta	saucer	o pires
large	grande	scarf	o lenço
larger	maior	scissors	a tesoura
laundry	a lavandaria	shampoo	o shampoo
leather	o cabedal	shaving cream	o creme de barbear
light	leve	shaving soap	o sabão de barbear
lighter (weight)	mais leve	shawl	o chaile
lighter (colour)	mais claro	shirt	a camisa
lighter flint	a pedra de isqueiro	shoes	os sapatos
		shoe-laces	os atacadores
lipstick	o batom de lábios	shop	a loja
long	comprido	shop assistant	o assistente
longer	mais comprido	short	curto
loose	solto	shorter	mais curto
looser	mais solto	shorts	calças
low	baixo	silk	a sêda
magazine	a revista	silver	a prata
manicure	a manicura	size	o tamanho
map	o mapa	skirt	a saia
matches	os fósforos	slip	a combinação
material	o tecido	slippers	as chinelas
nail	a unha	small	pequeno
nail-brush	a escova de unhas	smaller	mais pequeno
nail-file	a lima de unhas	soap	o sabonete
narrow	estreita	socks	as meias
narrower	mais estreita	spectacles	os óculos
necklace	o colar	stationer	a papelaria
needle	a agulha	stockings	as meias
newsagent	o quiosque	strap	a correia
newspaper	o jornal	string	o cordel
nightdress	a camisa de noite	strong	forte
nylons	as meias de nylon	stronger	mais forte
pale	pálido	suede	a pele de antilope

suit	o fato	tin	a lata
suitcase	a mala	tobacco	o tabaco
sun-lotion	o creme de sol	tobacconist	o tabaqueiro
spoon	a colher	toothbrush	a escova de
sun-glasses	os óculos de sol		dentes
suntan cream (oil)	o creme de bronzear	tooth paste	a pasta dentifrícia
		toy	um brinquedo
sweater	a camisola	trousers	as calças
sweets	os doces	umbrella	o guardachuva
tailor	o alfaiate	underwear	a roupa interior
tea	o chá	vacuum flask	a garrafa termos
thick	grosso	wallet	a carteira
thicker	mais grosso	watch	o relógio
thin	magro	wide	largo
thread	o fio	wider	mais largo
tie	a gravata	wine	o vinho
tight	apertado	writing-paper	o papel
tighter	mais apertado	zip	o fecho de correr

Sightseeing

What is there of interest to see?	O que há de interessante para ver?
Is there a tourist information bureau here?	Há aqui um centro de informações?
Is there an English-speaking guide?	Há um guia que fale inglês?
I don't want a guide	Não quero guia
I want to go to . . .	Quero ir a . . .
How much is this excursion?	Quanto é esta excursão?
Are there any boat trips?	Há excursões de barco?
How long does it take?	Quanto tempo dura?
What time does the trip begin?	A que horas começa a excursão?
When do I get back?	Quando estarei de volta?
We want to be together	Queremos estar juntos
Can I go in?	Posso entrar?
Is this the way to . . .?	É este o caminho para . . .?
How far is it from here to . . .?	A que distância fica daqui?
How long will it take?	Quanto tempo levará?
I want a quick look around the town	Quero fazer uma visita rápida à cidade
This (that) way	Por aqui (ali)
I am lost	Estou perdido

archaeology	a arqueologia	garden (botanical)	o jardim (botânico)
battlement	a ameia		
bridge	a ponte	garden (zoological)	o jardim (zoológico)
building	o edifício		
cable car	o teleférico	gate	o portão
castle	o castelo	gorge	o desfiladeiro
cathedral	a catedral	guide	o guia
church	a igreja	gulf	o golfo
city	a cidade	interpreter	o intérprete
coast	a costa	lake	o lago
excursion	a excursão	law courts	os tribunais de justiça
fountain	a fonte		
gallery (art)	a exposição (de quadros)	lighthouse	o farol
		monument	o monumento
gallery (museum)	o museu	mountain	a montanha
		mountain railway	o cabo teleférico

pottery	*a cerâmica*	street	*a rua*
rest, to	*descansar*	town hall	*a câmara municipal*
river	*o rio*		
ruins	*as ruínas*	valley	*o vale*
seat	*o banco*	village	*a aldeia*
square	*a praça*		

Sport

Do you play . . .?	*Joga . . .?*
May I join you?	*Posso tomar parte?*
Would you like to join in?	*Gostaria de tomar parte?*
Would you like a game of . . .?	*Quer jogar . . .?*
Well played!	*Bem jogado!*
Where is the swimming pool?	*Onde está a piscina?*
Can I hire a bathing costume and/or towel?	*Posso alugar um fato de banho e/ou uma toalha?*
Where are the tennis courts?	*Onde são os campos de tenis?*
Is there a golf course?	*Há um campo de golfe?*
Where can I fish?	*Onde posso pescar?*
I would like to water-ski	*Quero fazer esqui aquático*
What is the cost per tow?	*Quanto custa cada reboque?*
Can I have a motor boat?	*Posso alugar uma lancha?*
Can I launch a boat here?	*Posso lançar um barco aqui?*
I should like to hire a sailing boat	*Quero alugar um veleiro*
Where can I moor?	*Onde posso atracar?*
Can I hire the necessary equipment?	*Posso alugar o equipamento necessário?*
Where can I go horse riding?	*Onde posso montar a cavalo?*
Where (when) can I see horse racing?	*Onde (quando) posso ver corridas de cavalos?*
I want to climb the . . .	*Quero trepar o . . .*
Where can I find a guide?	*Onde posso encontrar um guia?*
What is the weather forecast?	*Qual é a previsão do tempo?*
I am only a beginner	*Eu sou um principiante*
Where (when) can I see a football match?	*Onde (quando) posso ver uma partida de futebol?*
What is the score?	*Qual é o resultado*

athletics	*o atletismo*	caddie	*o caddie*
billiards	*os bilhares*	golf club	*o taco*
boxing	*o pugilismo*	golf course	*o campo de golfe*
bowls	*as bolas*	green	*o relvado*
cycling	*o ciclismo*	hole	*o buraco pequeno*
darts	*os dardos*	miniature golf	*o mini-golfe*
football	*o futebol*	putt	*o putt*
fishing		**horse racing**	
bait	*a isca*	bet	*a aposta*
bait tin	*a lata de isco*	flat race	*a corrida plana*
fishing reel	*a bobina*	grandstand	*a bancada coberta*
fishing rod	*a vara*		
float	*a bóia*	horse	*o cavalo*
hook	*o anzol*	jockey	*o jóquei*
line	*a corda*	steeplechase	*a corrida de obstáculos*
spool	*o carreto*		
golf		tote	*o totalizador*
ball	*a bola*	**horse riding**	
bunker	*o buraco*	horse	*o cavalo*

jump	*o salto*	skis	*os esquis*
pony trekking	*montar num ponéi*	tow-rope	*a sirga*
rein	*a rédea*	**swimming**	
ride	*o passeio*	bathing costume	*o fato de banho*
saddle	*a sela*	dive	*mergulhar-se*
stirrup	*o estribo*	swim	*nadar*
sailing		swimming pool	*a piscina*
anchor	*a âncora*	**tennis**	
helm	*o leme*	balls	*as bolas*
lifejacket	*o cinto de salvação*	doubles	*a partida de pares*
		partner	*o parceiro*
mast	*o mastro*	player	*o jogador*
sails	*as velas*	racquet	*a raqueta*
water ski-ing		service	*o serviço*
water ski, to	*fazer esqui aquático*	singles	*jogo de singulares*
		tennis court	*o campo de ténis*
motor boat	*a lancha*		

Tipping

Is the service included?	*Está incluído o serviço?*
Keep the change	*Fique com o troco*
Tip	*A gorjeta*

Travel

Train/Bus

Can you help me with my luggage?	*Pode ajudar-me com a minha bagagem?*
I shall take this myself	*Eu levarei isto*
Don't leave this	*Não deixe isto*
Where is the . . .?	*Onde está o . . .?*
What is the fare to . . .?	*Qual é preço para . . .?*
Give me a first- (second-) class ticket for . . .	*Dê-me um bilhete de primeira (segunda) classe para . . .*
I want a sleeping-berth	*Quero um beliche (uma cama)*
I want to reserve a seat	*Quero reservar um lugar*
What time is the next (last) train for . . .?	*A que horas sai o último comboio para . . .?*
From which platform does it leave?	*De que plataforma sai?*
Where is the booking (inquiry) office?	*Onde é a bilheteira (informação)?*
Do you stop at . . .?	*Pára em . . .?*
Must I change for . . .?	*Tenho de mudar de combóio para . . .?*
Is this right for . . .?	*Está bem para . . .?*
Where (when) are the meals served?	*Onde (quando) servem as refeições?*
This seat is reserved	*Este lugar está reservado*
Someone has taken my seat	*Alguém ocupou o meu lugar*
Can you find me another seat?	*Pode encontrar-me outro lugar?*
Is this seat vacant?	*Está livre este lugar?*
This seat is (not) vacant	*Este lugar (não) está livre*
May I open (close) the window?	*Posso abrir (fechar) esta janela?*
Where is the toilet?	*Onde está a toilette?*
Where are we?	*Onde estamos?*
I want to put my luggage in the left luggage office	*Quero deixar a minha bagagem no depósito de bagagens*

How much do I owe you?	*Quanto devo?*
Taxi hire	
Is there a taxi?	*Há por aqui um taxi?*
I am going to . . .	*Vou para . . .*
Here is the address	*Aqui está o endereço*
I am in a hurry	*Estou com pressa*
Will you drive as quickly as possible	*Faça o favor de guiar o mais rápido possível*
Go more slowly	*Vá mais devagar*

airline office	*os escritórios da linha aérea*
airport	*o aeroporto*
arrival	*a chegada*
bag	*a mala*
berth	*a cama*
blanket	*o cobertor*
boat	*o barco*
booking-office	*a bilheteira*
bus	*o autocarro*
carriage (coach)	*a carruagem*
coach	*o autocarro*
compartment	*o compartimento*
communication cord	*o alarme*
connection	*a ligação*
Customs	*a alfândega*
Customs officer	*o empregado alfandegário*
departure	*a partida*
dining-car	*o vagão-restaurante*
door	*a porta*
driver	*o condutor/motorista*
entrance	*a entrada*
exit	*a saída*
fare	*o preço da viagem*
half-fare	*meio-bilhete*
inquiry office	*as informações*
journey	*a viagem*
label	*a etiqueta*
last	*último*
luggage	*a bagagem*
luggage-van	*o vagão de bagagem*

next	*próximo*
number	*o número*
passenger	*o passageiro*
passport	*o passaporte*
pillow	*a almofada*
platform	*o cais, a plataforma*
platform ticket	*o bilhete de cais (gare)*
port	*o pôrto*
porter	*o bagageiro*
railway	*a via férrea*
seat	*o lugar*
seat reservation	*a reserva de lugar*
smoking compartment	*o compartimento onde é permitido fumar*
station	*a estação*
station-master	*o chefe de estação*
stop	*a paragem*
subway	*o subterrâneo*
suitcase	*a mala*
taxi	*o táxi*
ticket, single (return)	*o bilhete, simples (de ida e volta)*
tickets, book of	*o caderno de bilhetes*
time-table	*o horário*
train	*o comboio*
tram	*o carro eléctrico*
trunk	*a mala*
waiting-room	*a sala de espera*
window	*a janela*